THE MEDIA WELFARE STATE

Joseph Turow
SERIES EDITOR

Broadcasting, Voice, and Accountability: A Public Interest Approach to Policy, Law, and Regulation
Steve Buckley, Kreszentia Duer, Toby Mendel, and Seán Ó Siochrú, with Monroe E. Price and Marc Raboy

Owning the Olympics: Narratives of the New China
Monroe E. Price and Daniel Dayan, editors

The Hyperlinked Society: Questioning Connections in the Digital Age
Joseph Turow and Lokman Tsui, editors

When Media Are New: Understanding the Dynamics of New Media Adoption and Use
John Carey and Martin C. J. Elton

Making News at *The New York Times*
Nikki Usher

The Media Welfare State: Nordic Media in the Digital Age
Trine Syvertsen, Gunn Enli, Ole J. Mjøs, and Hallvard Moe

DIGITALCULTUREBOOKS, an imprint of the University of Michigan Press, is dedicated to publishing work in new media studies and the emerging field of digital humanities.

The Media Welfare State

NORDIC MEDIA IN THE DIGITAL ERA

Trine Syvertsen, Gunn Enli, Ole J. Mjøs,
AND Hallvard Moe

The University of Michigan Press
ANN ARBOR

Published in the United States of America by
The University of Michigan Press
Manufactured in the United States of America
♾ Printed on acid-free paper

2017 2016 2015 2014 4 3 2 1

A CIP catalog record for this book is available from the British Library.

DOI: http://dx.doi.org/10.3998/nmw.12367206.0001.001

Library of Congress Cataloging-in-Publication Data

Syvertsen, Trine.
The media welfare state : Nordic media in the digital era / Trine Syvertsen, Gunn Enli, Ole J. Mjøs, and Hallvard Moe.
pages cm. — (The new media world)
Includes bibliographical references and index.
ISBN 978-0-472-07215-6 (hardcover : alk. paper) — ISBN 978-0-472-05215-8 (pbk. : alk. paper) — ISBN 978-0-472-12031-4 (e-book)
1. Mass media—Social aspects—Scandinavia. 2. Digital media—Social aspects—Scandinavia. 3. Public broadcasting—Scandinavia. 4. Mass media policy—Scandinavia. 5. Mass media and culture—Scandinavia. I. Enli, Gunn, 1970– II. Mjos, Ole J., 1970– III. Moe, Hallvard. IV. Title.
P92.S34.S97 2014
302.23'0948—dc23

2014002777

Contents

Acknowledgments

This is a cowritten monograph, and the authors have all taken part in developing the overall framework and main points of each chapter. Still, there has been a division of labor. Ole J. Mjøs had the original idea for the book, developed the initial synopsis together with Hallvard Moe, and coordinated the work from start to finish. He is the primary author of chapter 4 and contributed significantly to chapters 1 and 6. Trine Syvertsen played a leading role in the development and conceptualization of the overarching perspectives. She is the primary author of chapters 1 and 2 and contributed significantly to chapters 4, 5, and 6. Gunn Enli is the primary author of chapter 5 and contributed significantly to chapters 3, 4, and 6. Hallvard Moe is the primary author of chapter 3 and contributed significantly to chapters 1, 4, and 5.

We are thankful for the commitment and enthusiasm of Joseph Turow, the book series editor, and Tom Dwyer, our acquisitions editor at the University of Michigan Press. We would also like to thank Andrea Olson for coordinating the copyediting of the manuscript.

We are grateful to the two anonymous reviewers, whose critique and suggestions improved the overall quality of the book. Many have commented on and discussed unfinished chapters and papers, and we particularly wish to thank Espen Ytreberg, Vilde Schanke Sundet, Kari Karpinnen, and Henrik Søndergaard for valuable feedback. Thanks to Lene Vibeke Hansen and Chi-men Darbandi for much appreciated practical assistance. Thanks to the Department of Information Science and Media Studies, University of Bergen, for financial support. We also wish to express our thanks to Maury Saslaf for proofreading.

We sincerely hope that the book will be useful to students of Nordic media. Many students have read and discussed preliminary versions of the book. We would like to extend our warm thanks to students attending Nordic media and summer school courses at the University of Oslo and courses on the Norwegian media system at the University of Bergen. We alone bear the responsibility for the book's content, but we have been inspired and encouraged by your helpful comments along the way.

// ONE //

The Nordic Model and the Media Welfare State

The Nordic region is the northernmost part of Europe, consisting of Norway, Sweden, Finland, Denmark, and Iceland, with a total population of approximately 25 million. It is known for the Nobel Prize, furniture retailer giant IKEA, children's favorite LEGO, pop groups such as ABBA and A-ha, oil riches, salmon, fjords, saunas, and snowy mountains. But the states of this region are also known throughout the world for their peculiar way of organizing their societies. Taken together, the social and economic systems in these countries have become known as the Nordic Model, a welfare state system that aims at universal rights within societies with comparatively small class, income, and gender differences.

Within the Nordic region, a distinct organization of media and communications has evolved throughout the analogue era. A publicly supported but independent press has boasted the world's highest readership figures; publicly funded and owned broadcasters have contributed to building national identity and strived for enlightenment while maintaining a mass audience in the face of intense competition, and securing the entire population's access to high-speed Internet services has been a consensual political goal. Far-reaching state interventions and support schemes have been combined with a strong adherence to the principle of freedom of speech. The outcome is an adaptive public media sector with a high degree of legitimacy existing alongside domestically, and to some extent globally, successful commercial media and communication companies.

The existence of distinct and common features in Nordic media and communications has been pointed out in both academic and industry studies (see, e.g., Hallin and Mancini 2004; World Economic Forum 2012, xiii; Economist Intelligence Unit 2010, 2). Yet, very few studies, and this is particularly true for studies emerging from within the region, take a genuine Nordic perspective. To the degree that studies are concerned with more than one Nordic country or media sector the emphasis is just as much on national differences as on similarities within the region. Furthermore, since a Nordic perspective is rare, it is seldom asked whether the media and communication systems in the Nordic region develop along a different path than in other countries or regions. There is a tendency to assume that the strong transformative forces that impact on all media systems, such as globalization, marketization, and fragmentation, hit Nordic systems with broadly the same strength as in larger and more dominant countries.

We deny neither that there are great variations within and between Nordic countries, nor that the challenges to traditional media and regulatory models have been massive over the last decades. In several studies we ourselves have detailed how the media sector has been globalized (Mjøs 2010a, 2012), how competition policy and industrial policy have come to play a more important role in the field of media (Syvertsen 2004; Storsul and Syvertsen 2007; Moe 2012c), how the relationship between the state and public service broadcasters is changing due to convergence and competition (Moe 2009, 2010), and how a range of commercial reality formats have invaded Nordic screens (Enli 2008; Enli and McNair 2010). Yet, the main point of this book is not to emphasize how traditional features and principles of regulation are being undermined. Instead, we aim to test the argument that continuity is just as important as change within Nordic media. We hope to show that although both principles and practices of media policy and regulation are modified and changed, such principles and practices are also to a large degree reaffirmed, sustained, and strengthened in the digital age.

The book's premise is that the Nordic media and communication systems are distinct enough to stand out in the world and that this warrants attention from scholars and practitioners. We argue that the organization of media and communications in the Nordic countries rests on a combination of four principles or pillars, all of which continue to be present in the 21st century. These principles, which are expounded later in the chapter, are *universal services, editorial freedom, a cultural policy for the media;* and last, but not least, a tendency *to choose policy solutions that are consensual and durable, based on consultation with both public and private stakeholders.* We argue that these organizational principles support institutions and user patterns that bear resemblance to the socioeconomic and political institutions that usually define the Nordic welfare states. We call this the *Media Welfare State.*

This book introduces the concept of the Media Welfare State and elaborates on its key components. We trace the Media Welfare State's historical roots in the 19th and 20th centuries and discuss its evolvement and change in the digital age. Empirically, the book offers an updated scrutiny of major media institutions, tackling key developments within the sector, including digitalization, the growth of online and social media, digital television, and the establishment of international and in some instances global media and communication brands with Nordic origins, such as Nokia, Schibsted, and Modern Times Group. Theoretically, we argue that an understanding of public communications and the role played by media is crucial for grasping how the welfare state, or any other societal model for that matter, is constructed, interpreted, and sustained. From the beginning, media and communication systems have been vital building blocks of the welfare state, although their importance has increased as information and communication in the late 20th and early 21st centuries have come to permeate most aspects of social life. We aim to illustrate that media studies and welfare state studies would benefit from closer cooperation; while insight from media studies can contribute to a deeper understanding of why and how social systems evolve and change, media studies can benefit from connecting to broader theoretical paradigms and perspectives.

Before discussing the Nordic Model and the accompanying concept of the Media Welfare State, a few introductory words about the Nordic region are in order. The Nordic countries include the states of Norway, Sweden, Denmark, Finland, and Iceland, of which the first three are referred to as Scandinavia. The five countries have common historical roots and were even united in a single monarchy in the 15th and parts of the 16th centuries. Since 1917, the four larger countries have all been sovereign states (Iceland did not achieve full independence until 1944), but sovereign states with strong political, cultural, and economic cooperation, as illustrated by the Nordic Council for interparliamentarian collaboration, established in 1952, and the Council of Ministers, established in 1971. A passport union, a common labor market, and reciprocal social security benefits for Nordic citizens residing outside their home country were all in place in the 1950s, thus allowing Nordic people to move freely across borders decades before the European Union adopted similar policies. The Nordic countries have historically been culturally homogenous, with a border-crossing minority, the Sami people, in the north, and with a number of schemes for cultural and artistic cooperation. Norwegian, Swedish, and Danish are relatively similar Indo-European languages, and people in these three countries can understand each other and read each other's languages. Icelandic belongs to the same language group but is more difficult for the others to understand, while Sami and Finnish belong to the Finno-Ugric language group. Even if English functions as the lingua franca when representatives of all Nordic countries are present, much Nordic cooperation requires that people only speak their mother tongue.

Although the Nordic countries have much in common with other wealthy Western societies, they have more in common with each other. As noted by Andersen et al. (2007, 14):

> The Nordic countries tend to create a cluster of their own along many dimensions. Other European countries (notably the Netherlands and Austria) are often similar in certain respects, but in no important respect do we see an outlier among the Nordics.

The Nordic countries constitute a distinct cultural and geographical entity among the world's nations, and the countries also share a common political, social, and economic system epitomized in the concept of the Nordic Model.

The Nordic Model

The idea of a Nordic model of society originated in academia, but the concept is also used in other spheres of society, and politicians refer to it frequently. For instance, Halldór Ásgrímsson, the secretary general of the Nordic Council of Ministers, and Jan-Erik Enestam, the director of the Nordic Council, the interparliamentary body for pan-Nordic collaboration, boasted in unison in 2008: "The Nordic Model is a source of pride for the people of the region. We like the fact that it has become a recognizable concept, a 'brand' in international political debate" (Ásgrímsson and Enestam 2008, 5).

In such an offhand use, the term has desirable, yet vague, connotations. Although they have not always found what they have been searching for, governments around the world have looked to the Nordic Model as something to emulate and learn from (Da 2008; Alestalo, Hort and Kuhnle 2009, 25). Inside the region, the idea is so popular "that political parties have competed for the 'ownership' of the kind of political system and welfare state that the concept is seen to denote" (Alestalo, Hort, and Kuhnle 2009, 2). Of course, due to its social democratic connotations, controversy erupts around the model from time to time. For example, the leader of the Norwegian populist Progress Party, Siv Jensen, in 2013 denounced the Norwegian variant of the model and claimed that "models must never get in the way of common sense" (VGNett, 2013, authors' translation). Yet, the Populist Party also supports the basic welfare state elements that define the Nordic Model. Two years earlier, the Swedish Social Democrats sought patent protection on "The Nordic Model"—a move that triggered protest from the political right, as well as from the Nordic Council (Nordic Council 2012).

The Nordic Model (or, alternatively, a Scandinavian model of a specific welfare regime type) emerged from a series of comparative studies in the

1980s (Alestalo, Hort and Kuhnle 2009, 1). Historically, these studies traced the model to the last decades of the 19th century with the introduction of early social policy schemes, including social insurance laws, old-age pensions, and subsidies to voluntary sickness funds (Alestalo, Hort, and Kuhnle 2009, 10). Such developments laid the basis for a parallel flourishing of respect for individual liberty and traditions of collectivism and community within an ethnically homogenous population. Particularly since World War II, Nordic societies have stood out in the world through their ability to unite economic growth and competitiveness with a strong public sector, while promoting broad public participation in the economic and social spheres of society.

Different scholars emphasize somewhat different aspects when describing the Nordic Model. Some highlight the ambitious aims to combine an efficient market economy and growth with a stable labor market, equality in the distribution of resources, and a high level of social cohesion (Andersen et al. 2007, 11). The model is aimed at fostering democratic conditions, a high level of civic participation, and equality among its citizens. Andersen et al. (2007, 13–14) point to three cross-regional dimensions: a comprehensive welfare state; major public and private spending on human capital; and labor market institutions with significant labor unions, employer organizations, and considerable wage synchronization. In these descriptions, the development of a welfare state through substantial levels of taxation and an ambitious redistribution of wealth and resources, thereby creating a social safety net, free public education, and universal health services, is the institutional driving force behind the model (Andersen et al. 2007; Hilson 2008; Einhorn and Logue 2004; Vike 1996, 537; Erikson et al. 1987, vii).

The conviction that there is a specific Nordic Model, and that it is beneficial to the well-being of citizens, is also backed up with reference to other types of indicators. In a comparative study of the level of social trust in 60 countries, Delhey and Newton (2005) characterize the trust level in the Nordic countries as "exceptional." "Norway, Sweden and Denmark have the highest level of trust of any of our 60 nations. Finland and Iceland are not far behind," state the authors, who indicate several explanatory factors: "All five countries are Protestant, rich and ethnically homogenous, and have high good government scores" (320). In this study, social trust is defined as the belief that others will not deliberately or knowingly harm you if they can avoid it and will look after your interests if possible. While 6 out of 10 in Norway and Sweden believe that people can generally be trusted, less than 1 out of 10 in Turkey and Brazil holds this view (311). Furthermore, the Nordic countries belong to the group of countries classified by the United Nations Development Program as having a "very high human development." The index is popularly referred to as "The best countries in the world to live in" (BBC 2009). Norway topped the global list in 2011, as it has done nine times since the index was introduced in 1990, with the other Nordic countries also scoring high (UNDP 2011a, 2011b).

A specific Nordic (or social democratic) type of society also surfaces in broader comparative studies. For example, this is the case in Esping-Andersen's (1990) typology of welfare state variations, which argues that rather than being linearly distributed, welfare states are clustered by regime type and come in three versions: the liberal, the corporatist, and the social democratic. The first version describes societies that favor a strong free-market ideology, of which the United States is the prime example. Here, the state provides "modest universal social-insurance plans" and has put in place benefits that "cater mainly to a clientele of low-income" (Esping-Andersen 1990, 26). The second, the corporatist model, which is identified in countries such as Austria, France, Germany, and Italy, is more comprehensive, but still preserves social differences. Welfare state rights in these countries are "attached to class and status" (1990, 27).

The third category is the social democratic or universal model. Here, Sweden is the prime example, although the characteristics are present in all Nordic countries. Universalism implies that welfare state provisions include all, independent of class or status, and the welfare state is not seen as a passive safety net for the poor, but as a vehicle for active social transformation.

> Rather than tolerate a dualism between state and market, between working class and middle class, the social democrats pursued a welfare state that would promote an equality of the highest standards, not an equality of minimal needs as was pursued elsewhere. (Esping-Andersen 1990, 27)

An equality of the highest standards implies that public schools, health services, and pension schemes are well funded and constitute the main services to the population at large, while private services are more marginal and supplementary.

Hall and Soskice (2001) present an alternative typology of Western societies. Rather than focusing on the level of welfare state provisions, they classify economies on the level of firm structure and how firms interact with the state. In their model, Western economies are split into two main types, liberal market economies and coordinated market economies, in addition to a third more tentative category, which they label "Mediterranean" (8, 19–21). The Nordic countries are placed in the category of coordinated market economies along with Germany, Austria, Switzerland, the Netherlands, Belgium, and Japan: countries that also come close to the Nordic countries on several other indicators. In these countries, there is a higher degree of coordination and interdependence between individual firms, as well as more extensive coordination with the state, than in the liberal market economies. There is a coordinated labor market where trade unions have retained much of their historical importance, and key actors are encouraged "to engage in collective discussion and reach agreements with each other" (Hall and Soskice 2001, 11).

Based on the aforementioned classifications, the Nordic Model appears as either a specific type of society or as a subcategory of a broader corporatist model. In both cases, the Nordic system is often referred to as social democratic, thereby implying a high degree of egalitarianism and universalism. The system has been created with a transformative agenda, in which the ambition has not been to preserve differences of class and status, as in other corporatist countries, but to enroll everybody in the same social security and welfare state provisions, which encourage participation and inclusion of all citizens in the political and cultural public spheres. Within the mixed and open economies, public elements remain strong, and deliberation and coordination are encouraged in both the economy and elsewhere. As pointed out by Hall and Soskice: "Nations with a particular type of coordination in one sphere of the economy (. . .) tend to develop complementary practices in other spheres as well" (18).

The Nordic Model is generally described in rather positive terms and is often held out as an ideal, both inside and outside the region. This raises the issue of glorification: to what degree does the model present a romanticized version of life in the Nordic countries, glossing over difficult questions and internal tensions in order to create a global brand? In 2008, the Nordic Council of Ministers invited five international writers to cast a critical look at the Nordic Model, several of which address the issue of ideals vs. reality. Marie-Laure Le Foulon, a French journalist specializing in Nordic affairs, titles her contribution "Homo Nordicus, A Paradoxical Figure" and observes: "Living among the Nordics is like living with walking guilt complexes" (19). Although fascinated by the Nordic countries, which she sees as "clean" and "green" (25), she notes that life here "can be miserable" and cites "sporadic drinking bouts" and "unfathomable sadness" as features of the Nordic character.

"High suicide rates, binge drinking and a lack of social relations" is also cited as a Nordic characteristic by Spanish journalist Anxo Lamela Conde (2008, 55). Charles Ferro, an American author and journalist, titles his contribution "A Fragile Creature That Needs Care" and refers to the reactions he gets among Americans when he cites the Nordic taxation rate, "madness" and "a nightmare" (47). With a slight ironic twist, German foreign correspondent Siegfried Thielbeer asks: is the Nordic region a cozy and peaceful society? reminding us that for Social Democrats and Socialists in Germany, as elsewhere, the Nordic societies symbolized "the realization of the old dreams of the working class" for many years. People of the Nordic countries were generally perceived as "peace-loving, rejecting all forms of militarism" (2008, 59), although Thielbeer matter-of-factly notes that this perception "was naturally flawed" (60).

Contributions such as these represent a welcome correction to what is not just conceptualized as a political system, but "a philosophy ingrained in the Nordic soul" (Ferro 2008, 45). The contributions grasp the strong individualism and relatively weaker family, social, and religious ties that tend to characterize people in the North (Vike 1996, 547), as well as the aspects of the Nordic Model, where the image exceeds reality. Still, it is also worth noting that observers who are specifically requested to be critical consider Nordic societies and mentalities to have a distinct character, epitomized in the concept of the Nordic Model.

The Nordic Model—Still Relevant?

The question remains as to whether a model that was detected through comparative analyses in the 1980s continues to be relevant in the 21st century. There is indeed a certain dated feel to some descriptions—for example, the widespread references to how social democrats built the welfare state (see, e.g., Esping-Andersen 1990, 27). Social democracy enjoyed unparalleled strength in the Nordic countries in the decades following World War II, but its hegemony was challenged in the 1980s. Historians point out how the dominant "social-democratic order" gradually gave way to "the era of the market" (Furre 1991, 421). "The three decades from the early 1960s to the end of the 1980s were the golden age of the Nordic welfare state," admit Alestalo, Hort, and Kuhnle (2009, 15; see also Christiansen and Markkola 2006, 21). Three more decades have passed since this golden age, and one may ask whether the significant social changes that have taken place have reduced the model's value as an explanatory tool.

Perhaps the most important question concerns whether the global move toward neoliberalism has undermined the Nordic welfare state. Neoliberal thought surfaced strongly from the late 1970s, influencing the agenda of conservative and right-wing parties worldwide. The result was a move toward a reduced national regulation of industry and labor markets, the privatization of health care and education, and the curbing of public spending. The implications have been profound for individual citizens, as Davis (2009, 3) argues in the US case: "The bonds between employees and firms have loosened, while the economic security of individuals is increasingly tied to the overall health of the stock market."

Nonetheless, the impact of neoliberalism has not been homogenous across the world (Harvey 2005, 13). Also in the Nordic countries, party politics took a turn to the right in the 1980s. The result was a changed state, viewed by some as a radical shift that turned the welfare state toward a "competition state" (Pedersen 2011, on Denmark). Still, outright neoliberalism did not take hold, at least not in the larger countries. The dominant parties on the right committed themselves to supporting the welfare state in the 1950s and 1960s, and since that time, the welfare state has to a large degree been a shared political project (Mjøset 2011, 391). New right-wing parties with a populist agenda surfaced in the region in the 1970s, initially mobilizing against state bureaucracy and high taxes, but these parties also gradually committed themselves to the welfare state, instead making the struggle against immigration their key mobilizing cause (2011, 411). As Kjølsrød (2003) points out in the Norwegian case, shifting governments have felt responsible for the welfare state throughout the entire postwar period. The system has been backed up by "stable political ambitions with broad support across party lines" (Kjølsrød 2003, 184; authors' translation). The only exception to this rule was in the smallest Nordic country of Iceland, where neoliberal ideology came to have a strong influence from the mid-1990s (Mjøset 2011, 411).

Neoliberalism is not the only force that has been held out as a potential challenge to the Nordic Model. Indeed, if one anchors the Nordic Model in the social democratic era of the early postwar years, all later developments may be perceived as "challenges" to the model. Many articles and books on the welfare state and the Nordic Model are implicitly or explicitly structured in this fashion: first, the core elements of the model are presented, then a number of challenges are discussed, and then comes the question of whether the model can adapt and survive (see, e.g., Andersen 2008a, 2008b; Alestalo, Hort, and Kuhnle 2009).

In addition to neoliberalism three such challenges are emphasized in the literature, with the first and most important being the force of globalization. For example, "Can the Scandinavian Model Adapt to Globalization?" ask Einhorn and Logue (2004), who discuss the difficulty of upholding a welfare state with specific and tangible characteristics in the face of integration, standardization, and interdependence (Einhorn and Logue 2004, 502; see also Alestalo, Hort, and Kuhnle 2009, 19). Changing demographics is another much focused on challenge, particularly the rise of the aging population, which implies that the number of dependent people (those receiving benefits) is growing at a faster rate than the proportion of employed (those paying taxes) (Andersen 2008b, 47; Andersen et al. 2007, 20–21). The demographic challenge includes the rise of an immigrant population, which is seen as both a challenge to social equality (most immigrants are working class) and a challenge in the sense that the number of beneficiaries of the welfare system may outnumber the contributors (Alestalo, Hort, and Kuhnle 2009, 17; Andersen

2008b, 61). The third challenge is political and concerns the cohesion, legitimacy, and governability of the welfare state. As the population becomes increasingly fragmented and heterogeneous, support for the welfare state may wane. Furthermore, the twin processes of globalization and European integration may lead to difficulties in upholding an ambitious welfare system in one country or region (Alestalo, Hort, and Kuhnle 2009).

These challenges are real enough and confront political systems worldwide. Indeed, there is a debate in all Nordic countries on how to sustain the welfare state in the face of globalization, aging, immigration, and European integration. The fear that the welfare state may be overstretched, that the demands on it have become too great and the contributors too few, gives rise to numerous public commissions and policy measures. Still, it is not adequate to simply perceive such forces as new challenges imposed on the system from outside. International constraints and possibilities, demographic change, and questions of legitimacy and cohesion have all been part and parcel of the welfare state since its conception and have been dealt with through varying political, social, and economic measures. For example, as Andersen et al. (2007, 12) note, globalization "has been the very basis of the growth in productivity and living standards which the Nordics have achieved." Within the Nordic welfare states, there has always been a combination of protective policies and defending internal coherence and solidarity, with relatively open economies and a high level of international participation and exchange.

In this light, the Nordic Model should be seen as a dynamic rather than dated construct, in addition to a construct that must be examined anew by historians and social scientists in light of contemporary societal development. As Halldór Ásgrímsson, secretary general of the Nordic Council of Ministers, and Jan-Erik Enestam, the director of the Nordic Council, stated in unison in 2008, the Nordic Model "is and has always been a work in progress" (Ásgrímsson and Enestam 2008, 5). How this work progresses, however, is not only dependent on economic and social features; it is also dependent on the Nordic countries' organization of their media and communication systems.

The Nordic Model—A Media-Free Society?

The literature on the welfare state is comprehensive and covers many aspects of social and economic life. Yet, one aspect is curiously absent—namely, the role of media and communication systems. As reviewed here, the literature on the Nordic Model lacks references to this central realm of political, cultural, and social life.

This goes for key collected volumes—for example: *Normative Foundations of the Welfare State: The Nordic Experience* (Kildahl and Kuhnle 2005); *The Scan-*

dinavian Model: Welfare States and Welfare Research (Erikson et al. 1987); *Welfare Trends in the Scandinavian Countries* (Hansen et al. 1993); *Welfare States in Transition: National Adaptations in Global Economies* (Esping-Andersen 1996); *Survival of the European Welfare State* (Kuhnle 2000); *The Nordic Model of Welfare: A Historical Reappraisal* (Christiansen et al. 2006). It is also true for articles discussing the conditions for the Nordic Model such as by Alestalo, Hort, and Kuhnle (2009).

Some contributions made by communication scholars do attempt to bridge the gap, including Manuel Castells and Pekka Himanen's (2002) *The Information Society and the Welfare State: The Finnish Model*. This country study of Finland introduces the concept of the "informational welfare state" as a way of describing "a welfare state that forms a virtuous circle with the informational economy" (2002, 87). On the one hand, Finland's information society provides the financial basis of the country's welfare state. On the other hand, the Finnish welfare state's public services provide "a sustainable social dimension" (2002, 87–88) to the competitive and globalized information economy (2002, 89). Furthermore, the concept of the "informational welfare state" includes both the social uses (see, e.g., "social hackerism" [2002, 96–100]) and the utilization of information technology to reform and develop the structures and services of the welfare state "through a more dynamic network organization" (2002, 90, 90–102). While this study provides much needed insights into the relationship between media and communications and the welfare state, it is limited to one country and therefore does not include a Nordic perspective. Its main focus is on communications technology as a vehicle to develop and reform the components, organization, and productivity of the welfare state, rather than on the media as a welfare state system.

The absence of references to the role of media and communications in mainstream Nordic welfare state literature is peculiar for several reasons, the first being that media and communication systems by themselves constitute important institutions in modern societies. The main infrastructures of public communication can all be traced back to the 19th and early 20th centuries, the same period when the social policy foundations of the welfare state were established. From the beginning, social democratic movements paid intense attention to communication and media, and both the party press and the public broadcasting institutions were perceived as crucial vehicles to achieve the aims of the welfare state. Moreover, key political figures have occupied positions as newspaper editors or director generals of the broadcasting institutions (Slagstad 1998, 432ff.; Bastiansen and Dahl 2003, 270ff.). From early on, postal systems, which were crucial to the distribution of newspapers, were organized as public services, as were telecommunication networks, which later would play a critical role in turning the Nordic countries into advanced information societies. In the interwar period, radio was institutionalized as public service monopolies in all Nordic countries, and this was extended to television in the 1950s and 1960s. During the "golden age" of the welfare state, the early postwar years, people in each Nordic country watched and listened to much the same content on very few (state-owned) channels, a feature that contributed to the homogeneity of culture and perspectives. In later decades, the social forces of marketization, globalization, and changing demographics have all impacted on media and communications structures in ways that are also relevant for—and have consequences for—other welfare state institutions. Thus, media and communication constitute essential elements in the historical construction of the welfare state, while also interpreting and reflecting its adaption and change in recent decades.

The second reason why communication should be included in welfare state studies is that communication is vital for legitimacy. As we have seen, social scientists studying the Nordic Model are concerned with the normative foundations of the welfare state, the legitimacy of its social provisions, and the possibility that the values necessary to sustain the model may be in a state of flux (Kildahl and Kuhnle 2005; Andersen 2008b, 47; Alestalo, Hort, and Kuhnle 2009). Yet, there is little mention in the literature as to how norms and values are sustained, debated, and negotiated—all crucial tasks of the media and communication system. Kjølsrød mentions three theories from welfare state literature as to how a system based on the heavy taxation of every household may be legitimated (2003, 185). The first is that citizens make a rational choice to support welfare state solutions as a form of personal insurance system, the second is that people support the welfare state out of a sense of solidarity with others, and the third is based on self-interest; in a universalist system, a large proportion of the population either benefit directly from the welfare state or work in professions that benefit from, or administer, welfare state provisions. These explanations are of course relevant and valuable, yet it is curious how the support for the welfare state is allegedly based on each citizen making a rational, ideological, or self-interested choice. There is a conspicuous lack of references to public debate or the public sphere, or to how ideologies and rationalities are disseminated, challenged, or sustained.

Some books and articles do refer to agencies of socialization and mobilization, although these are limited to schools, the church, and political parties. Kildahl and Kuhnle (2005, 25) suggest that the broad support for universalism was due to a "long, dynamic argumentative process," seeing that the political parties are the key actors. This may well be true, but political parties rarely communicate directly and unmediated with the electorate. What political parties have ample opportunities to do, however, is to influence the setup of the media system, safeguarding that diverse voices and viewpoints are present, among them voices that may be expected to be broadly in favor of universalism and welfare state solutions. In a publicly regulated system, populism can be kept in check, and the media can to a larger degree be held accountable to society than in a purely market-driven system.

The third reason why media and communication are important for our understanding of the welfare state has to do with social cohesion. The media and public communication systems are frequently understood as a form of "social glue," cf. Benedict Anderson's (1992, 25) argument about the nation as "an imagined community." In his conception, the experience of belonging to a nation is not based on face-to-face interaction between its members, and not even on personal experiences, but on a mental image of affinity in part sustained and upheld by a public communication system. Feelings of solidarity, belonging, inclusion, and exclusion in society are not exclusively or even primarily based on each individual's experience, but instead on a complex interplay of narratives that, to a large extent, are transmitted through media. Even so, the media may also frame social problems in a way that increases divisions and increases feelings of alienation among social groups. As the social base of society becomes more diverse and fragmented, public communication systems remain important agents of cohesion and social bonding.

The aim of this book is to draw the media and communication systems more firmly into the field of welfare state studies. By this, we do not mean to go into detailed analysis of how various media support or confront central welfare state aims and how media coverage influences the public's view, even though such studies are clearly valuable (see, e.g., Knudsen 2013). Rather, our argument regards media policy and organization. On a basic level, we argue that studies of the Nordic Model and the welfare state are simply incomplete without an accompanying discussion of its media and communications component. On a higher level of complexity, we contend that it is difficult to understand how the welfare state is legitimated, and how cohesion and trust are sustained, without an understanding of the principles that govern systems of public communications.

Societal Models and Media Models

Within the field of media and communication studies, it is commonplace to analyze media systems as a reflection of the social systems of which they are a part. Early contributions such as *Four Theories of the Press* (Siebert, Peterson, and Schramm 1956) divided media systems into four categories, each reflecting an ideal type of society: Authoritarian, Libertarian, Socially Responsible, and Soviet Communist. *Four Theories of the Press* remains a classic text within media studies and is frequently referred to, but it has also been widely criticized for its simplicity, lack of empirical basis, and Cold War defense of liberalism (see Hardy 2008, 11ff.; Nordenstreng 2006; and Hallin and Mancini 2004, 9–10, for recent critiques).

However, similar elements do appear in more solid theoretical constructs. Gerhard Vowe (1999) takes the idealized and recurring themes of freedom, security, and equality from political philosophy and employs them as labels for media policy. Freedom is emblematic for the liberal systems of the United States, Australia, and Britain, whereas the most important value in Austria and Germany is security. These countries are both corporatist democracies focused on protecting more or less fragile social structures from inner and outer threats, while in the Nordic countries, which Vowe labels social democratic, the key value is equality. Although Vowe's analysis is based on a different principle of classification, the resulting categories are similar to the ones found in Esping-Andersen (1990). Both Vowe and Esping-Andersen distinguish between corporatist systems and social democratic systems, identifying the Nordic countries as the prime example of the latter.

In *Comparing Media Systems: Three Models of Media and Politics* (2004), Daniel C. Hallin and Paolo Mancini also divide media systems into three types. The outcome of their division is more similar to Hall and Soskice (2001), also quoted earlier, in that they place the Nordic countries together with other corporatist countries. Hallin and Mancini distinguish between the North Atlantic or liberal model, the Mediterranean or polarized pluralistic model, and the North/Central European democratic corporatist model, with the latter model including the Nordic countries (excluding Iceland), Germany, the Netherlands, Austria, Belgium, and Switzerland (Hallin and Mancini 2004, 11, 89ff.).

The third category describes well some of the vital ingredients of the Nordic media systems, most notably the importance of a mass circulation press, the historical shift from party newspapers toward a neutral commercial press, a strong institutionalized professionalism, and wide-ranging, but legally limited, state intervention. The much-cited study is based on empirical research, and one of its advantages is that it shows how significant components have been reinterpreted and modified under changing circumstances.

Hallin and Mancini's models are considered the most authoritative within comparative media studies. Yet, their model-building has also been widely criticized: the specific labels and categories have been disputed, along with the temporal dimension (Hardy 2012). Their relative disregard of factors that could differentiate systems, ranging from country and market size (e.g., Hardy 2012) to the role of religious institutions (Couldry 2007), has also been duly discussed. Yet others have sought to extend the scope to other parts of the world (e.g., Voltmer 2008; see Hallin and Mancini 2012a) and stressed the need for more in-depth analysis of specific countries, aiming at exposing differences within generally similar categories (e.g., Humphreys 2012). The comparative efforts of Hallin and Mancini and others have also inspired Nordic scholars (Strömbäck, Ørsten, and Aalberg 2008 on political communication; Nord 2008 on press and broadcast regulation and structures; Kjær and Slaatta 2007 on business journalism).

For a study such as the present one, another limitation is more pressing: Hallin and Mancini's focus on traditional news media, predominantly the printed press. This limitation has two separate consequences. First, forms of media content that fall outside the news category tend to be ignored. This might not be a problem within the field of political communication, where the contribution arguably has received the most traction. For studies with a wider perspective, however, it makes less sense to make do with news only, as it limits the validity of the models, as well as the richness of the empirical analysis (e.g., Hardy 2008).

Second, by concentrating on the printed press along with traditional broadcast media, the model-building does not reflect the changes in a digital era. Though the importance of new technologies might have been harder to assess in 2004, Hallin called the Internet and digital media in general "a big hole" in the book (in Moe and Sjøvaag 2009, 137). The decade that has passed since the publication, though, has seen contributions retaining a focus on traditional media (e.g., Hardy 2008; also Hallin and Mancini 2012a). This is also the case for recent contributions with a Nordic perspective (Strömbäck, Ørsten and Aalberg 2008).

Any study of media and communication systems today needs to take Internet and digital media into account. Doing so does not invalidate the categories; indeed, more recent attempts at model-building that include digital media point to distinguishing and unifying characteristics of the Nordic countries. In her study of how the Internet has been encouraged and implemented in different countries, Ursula Maier-Rabler (2008) sketches four ideal types of "information cultures": Catholic-feudalistic, Protestant-enlightened, socialist-centralistic, and socio-democratic. The socio-democratic information culture characterizes the Nordic countries and parts of the Benelux area. The key value distinguishing the social democratic type from the three other cultures is that "information is a precondition for the political emancipation of the individual" (2008, 58). Although parts of the Benelux area are included in the social democratic type, Maier-Rabler allocates the Nordic countries a special place and claims that Scandinavia has the most advanced constitutional framework delineating the free access to information (Maier-Rabler 2008, 58; see also chap. 2).

The main conclusion to be drawn from a review of societal and media models is that the Nordic countries tend to be singled out as a special case—

either placed in a category of their own or treated as a subcategory within a larger type. This is the case whether we look only at traditional media or if we integrate analyses of digital media and genres beyond hardcore news. In our description of the Nordic media systems as a Media Welfare State, we discuss the Internet not as a new, isolated technology, but ask how its expansion, as well as the general trend toward convergence, contributes to transformation of all other aspects of media: the printed press, broadcasting, media use, and operations of media companies. In the same way as the Nordic states cluster on a number of social and economic variables, they cluster on variables related to media and communication—both traditional and newer forms. We clearly acknowledge that there are differences between Nordic countries and that in some respects individual countries are similar to those outside the region. Yet, the clustering is distinct enough so that it is worth testing the idea of a Media Welfare State, a set of organizational principles or pillars that function in much the same way as the more general social and economic provisions of the welfare state.

The Media Welfare State

The model of a Media Welfare State explored in this book is based on a combination of reactive and proactive measures. The principles can in part be understood as a series of responses to historical forces that have been seen to constrain and negatively affect the media system and in part be understood as a battery of proactive public policy measures.

Four social forces in particular have been perceived as threats to a media system based on welfare state principles. The first is *authoritarianism*, or direct state influence over content. As we see in later chapters, Nordic policymakers explicitly rejected the idea of state-controlled media in the 19th and 20th centuries. The second force is that of *marketization*, both structurally and in terms of content. In the Nordic countries, unmediated market forces have been perceived to create unequal access, as well as reducing diversity and driving quality downward. The third force is that of international standardization, more recently termed *globalization*. We will show that there has been a strong desire to protect national and regional culture, identity, and language from international commercial pressures. The fourth force to be counteracted is that of *social fragmentation*, as Nordic policymakers have not easily accepted cultural and social divisions based on wealth, geography, age, ethnicity, or religious affiliations.

The purpose of identifying these forces is to demonstrate that political intervention in the media system does not appear out of nowhere, but is instituted after a deliberative process in order to deal with perceived problems

TABLE 1.1. The Four Pillars of the Media Welfare State[a]

1: An organization of vital communication services that underscores their character as *public goods*, with extensive cross-subsidies and obligations toward universality.
2: A range of measures used to institutionalize *freedom from editorial interference* and self-governance in day-to-day operations.
3: A *cultural policy that extends to the media* in the form of content obligations and support schemes that aim to secure diversity and quality.
4: A preference for consensual solutions that are durable and involve *cooperation between main stakeholders:* the state, media and communication industries and the public.

[a]See the appendix for an extended version of table 1.1.

and challenges (Syvertsen 2004, 62). Problems and challenges associated with these forces are recurring and emerge anew in the digital age. In order to handle them, policymakers and media institutions may choose from a catalogue of measures developed in the analogue era and modified throughout media history.

These measures fall into two types: (1) there are specific regulatory instruments, such as press subsidies or the broadcasting monopoly, that are applied to singular media at specific times. Many such instruments are discussed in coming chapters, and we also show how specific regulations are changed and adapted to suit new times; (2) there are general policy solutions and principles that govern different media and communication sectors across historical periods that are more durable and consistent. On the basis of the analysis presented in this book and on literature covering Nordic media systems, we suggest that four such general principles and ways of conducting policy are recurring in Nordic media and communications (see, e.g., Hadenius, Weibull, and Wadbring 2011; Maier-Rabler 2008; Syvertsen 2004; Jensen 1997, 2003; Duelund 2003). We label these the four principles or pillars of the Media Welfare State:

In the same way as a key ideal of the Nordic Model is universal social provisions, the first pillar of the Media Welfare State is *universally available communication systems*. In the 19th century, educational and communication services were organized as public services in all Nordic countries, hence laying the foundations for both mass democracy and an egalitarian media consumption pattern. The Nordic countries stand out as early proponents of universal education, safeguarding literacy for women as well as men, with both postal and telecommunications systems organized with a view toward achieving equal access. In the 20th century, both radio and television were instituted as public monopolies with the same obligations. Although the broadcasting, telecommunication, and postal monopolies were all abandoned in the 1980s and 1990s, a strong obligation toward universal services remained: In the

1990s, selected commercial broadcasters were obliged to be universally available, whereas in the 2000s the same principle was applied to digital terrestrial television networks. Universal services are not specific to Nordic societies, though the principle in these states has been applied on a rather grand scale. In the 21st century, both public investment in infrastructures and ambitious universal service obligations are among the explanations for why the Nordic countries have placed themselves in the global lead as far as Internet and broadband coverage is concerned.

The second pillar of the Media Welfare State, *institutionalized editorial freedom*, is not a trait specific to Nordic societies. However, this principle also has a comparatively stronger position in the Nordic region than in many other countries and regions, as the Nordic countries were among the first to institutionalize press freedom; indeed, Sweden prides itself on having the world's oldest constitutional provision of freedom of expression, dating back to 1766, 20 years before France and the United States. The editorial freedom in Nordic media shows an uninterrupted history and continuity in peacetime. This long history of press freedom—a freedom that is still being respected—is held out as a key characteristic of the Nordic region based on the comparative analysis by Hallin and Mancini (2004, 145). The early autocratic rulers of the Nordic monarchies introduced strict penalties for public criticism, but parliamentary governments in the last century, whether social democrat, centrist, or conservative, have respected the media's editorial independence. The Nordic countries continue to distinguish themselves on global press freedom indexes in the 21st century, which is particularly notable since the state is so involved with the media sector.

The third pillar, *the presence of an extensive cultural policy for the media*, is crucial in order to understand the fundamental setup of the Media Welfare State. Whereas universal service provisions predominantly have to do with infrastructure, and editorial independence is a negative freedom—a freedom from interference—cultural policy measures for the media are set up to positively influence media content. Broadly speaking, the objective of such measures has been to modify the influence of market forces, thus countering the strong influx of standardized and global mass culture in the 20th century. The cultural policy for the media was initially developed for public service radio in the interwar period; from the beginning, the nascent monopolies were conceived as agents of enlightenment and nation-building. The principles were extended to television in the 1950s and 1960s, and three decades later selected commercial broadcasters were obliged to offer cultural, informational, and minority content in return for financial and distributional privileges. Press subsidies, which arrived in the 1950s, are clearly a product of cultural policy, as the state intervened in a free-market structure to safeguard that different views and opinions should also be published regionally and locally. Cultural policy measures are not exclusive to these media, but also apply to films and books and, to some degree, new media as well, such as the Norwegian support schemes for computer games (St. meld. 14, 2007/2008).

The cultural policy for the media has enjoyed broad support and has also corresponded well with the editorial goals of the mainstream media. Both within the press and broadcasting, there has been strong support for the view that the media should appeal to all and should inform and enlighten the population at large, as neither content nor consumption has shown strong divisions along class and gender lines. Still, the cultural policy for the media has not gone unopposed. For example, the Swedish Modern Times Group, one of the largest international media companies with Nordic origins, has openly confronted public regulation and media support systems and has pursued an aggressively competitive corporate strategy in press, radio, and television. However, their approach has been exceptional in the Nordic context, as most media corporations have had more to gain from a more supportive attitude toward cultural policy aims.

This leads us to the fourth pillar of the Media Welfare State, *consensual policy-making and compromises between key stakeholders*. A defining characteristic of the welfare state is often seen as "stateness": a persistent feature in which the relationship between the state and the people is "a close and positive one" (Alestalo, Hort, and Kuhnle 2009, 2) and where the state is perceived "as an agency through which society can be reformed" (Korpi 1978, 48, cited in Alestalo, Hort, and Kuhnle 2009, 2). Although the media sector displays the same "stateness" as the Nordic Model at large, we would argue that perhaps a more distinguishing trait is the extent to which private and commercial operators have accepted and taken part in state-regulated schemes and policies and found them beneficial for their own corporate interest. Consensual and pragmatic policy formation is a general feature of the Nordic Model that dates back to the interwar period, reflecting both the compromises between labor and capital and the fact that most governments have been party coalitions (Alestalo, Hort, and Kuhnle 2009, 7). At each crucial moment in media history, we see a preference for consensual and cooperative policies, rather than clean-cut statist or market-led solutions, an observation that underscores Hall and Soskice's (2001) point about coordinated market economies. Nonetheless, cooperation does not mean that private companies are overly restricted in their operations or that the interests of state and industry merge. As we have noted, the Nordic states have always had relatively open economies, allowing Nordic companies to take advantage of global market opportunities, while at the same time benefitting from protective policies intended to defend domestic media from the twin pressures of marketization and globalization.

These four pillars or principles are general policy solutions that constitute the basis for the Media Welfare State. Following this brief sketch, the pillars are elaborated and discussed in the chapters to come, where we also discuss challenges to Nordic media systems and inherent differences within the Nordic region, as well as the adaptions and modifications in the light of social and media change.

Summary and Plan for the Book

The purpose of this book is twofold. The first main purpose is to introduce the concept of the Media Welfare State and argue for its importance in studies of the Nordic Model. The Media Welfare State is understood as a combination of both reactive and proactive elements and is defined as resting on four key pillars: *Universal and egalitarian services*, *freedom from editorial interference*, *a cultural policy that extends to the media*, and *a preference for solutions that are durable and involve cooperation between all main stakeholders*. We argue that there are profound similarities between the socioeconomic features of the Nordic welfare states on the one hand and the cultural and informational features on the other.

The second main purpose of the book is to discuss how Nordic media and communications adapt and change in the digital age. While it is difficult to identify precisely when the digital era begins, our main focus is on the period from the late 1990s and throughout the first decade of the 21st century. From the late 1990s, digitalization began to affect all media: the Internet took off after the introduction of the first web browser in 1993, mobile telephones were about to become commonplace, and the first digital satellite and cable television channels were launched with the promise of greater choice. As the digital age evolves, new services increase the public's choice and participation; providers from outside the region target Nordic users, while companies from within the region venture outside their borders. As all parts of media and communications move from analogue to digital technology, both principles and practices of media governance are adapted and modified in various ways. Still, we argue that there are strong signs of continuity as well as change; overall principles and user patterns are to a large degree maintained and fortified. What we have identified as the pillars of the Media Welfare State also retain their position as key shaping forces of Nordic media and communications in the digital era.

Methodologically, the book draws on analyses of institutional, political, and state documents and on national and international statistics, as well as on research-based studies and comparative works. In addition, the book accesses highly updated sources, including news items, corporate and public information, and socioeconomic information available in the public domain.

A methodological note of caution concerns the availability of statistics.

Each Nordic country has high quality and frequently updated media statistics. Since our purpose is in part to describe Nordic characteristics insofar as they differ from other regions and countries, we have based our analysis less on statistics from individual countries and more on comparative studies. The implication is that the data are not always updated and do not always include all Nordic countries. We try to clarify shortcomings as we go along, yet it is important to point out that not all our observations build on equally strong empirical evidence. Reputable studies from international agencies used in the book include Eurostat (2011), Nordicom, the International Telecommunications Union (2011, 2012), the Economist Intelligence Unit (2010), the World Economic Forum (2012), the United Nations Development program (2011a, 2011b), the International Federation of Phonographic Industry (2010), Nordvisjon (2012), and the World Association of Newspapers (2005). Statistics and other evidence from individual countries are used to illustrate specific cases.

The book contains six chapters.

Chapter 2 deals with *media use.* Media user patterns are important as an indication of how the principles of the Media Welfare State work on the ground, so to speak. Based on comparative European, and in some cases global, statistics, the chapter identifies similar patterns of media use across the Nordic countries. Nordic users have traditionally been high consumers of newspapers, other print and factual media, and public service broadcasting. Although there are changes, these basic features continue in the 21st century. The chapter further discusses the developments whereby the Nordic countries have turned into some of the world's most advanced information economies, with early and high penetration of mobile phones, Internet, and broadband. In comparison with others, the people of the Nordic countries are particularly interested in online news; they are among the world's most active users of Facebook and download and purchase large quantities of cultural and informational material off the Internet. The chapter discusses whether the fragmentation of media output is reflected in an increasing fragmentation of media consumption. Although there are changes, the chapter concludes that there is no strong evidence that information gaps are widening and also concludes that there is a continuation of the commonality and egalitarianism that have traditionally characterized media use in the Nordic region.

Chapter 3 focuses on *the press.* Historically, the printed press has played a crucial role in the establishment of the Nordic countries as open, democratic societies. Within the newspaper sector there has been strong support for the view that the media should appeal to all and should inform and enlighten the population at large, and consumption of newspapers has been high in all social groups. The number of locally, regionally, and nationally printed newspapers in the region is generally higher than in other regions. Compared with other countries and regions, the Nordic press has had a long and strong history of editorial freedom and well-functioning self-regulatory institutions. Still, the Nordic region is not unaffected by global transformations and the decline in traditional printed newspapers, and the chapter investigates both the rise of free newspapers and the transformation to online news production. The chapter shows that the rise of global media and increased public involvement pose challenges to the traditional conception of publishing, but also that there is continued commitment, although the strength of the commitment varies, to continue the system of public press support to counteract what is seen as the negative influence of the market.

Chapter 4 deals with *public service broadcasting*. More than any other media, the public service broadcasters embody the principles of what we have termed the Media Welfare State. We show how public service broadcasters in the Nordic countries were set up as universal services in the interwar period and how their funding systems with no advertising and license fees were intended to protect them against pressures from both the state and the market. The public service broadcasters have served each Nordic nation with high quality and diverse output, and we show how their adaptive approach to enlightenment has ensured that they remain popular even in the face of intense competition. Also in their response to other challenges, the public service broadcasters have been adaptive and flexible, and they have retained a high degree of both public and political legitimacy. In the chapter we pay particular emphasis to the start-up of niche services such as children's channels and the transformation of the public corporations into multiplatform enterprises. Throughout the chapter we compare the Nordic public service broadcasters with those of other regions and countries and also make comparisons between the individual Nordic institutions.

Chapter 5 explores the role of *private media and communications companies*. A hallmark of the Nordic welfare states is the successful public-private mix, yet most studies with a welfare state perspective center on state institutions. This chapter focuses on understanding the role of private media and communications companies through the study of three cases, representing different types of corporations: *Nokia*, the Finnish telecommunications hardware manufacturer, once the world's largest producer of mobile telephones; *Schibsted*, the Norwegian internationally expanding publishing house and a global leader in online classifieds; and the Swedish company *Modern Times Group*, an international player in television, radio, and free newspapers. The chapter maps the development of the three companies within the Nordic region and internationally and discusses their expansion in relation to the policy solutions and regulatory systems of the Media Welfare State. Although the chapter touches on several aspects of the Media Welfare State, the emphasis is on the fourth pillar, the tendency toward consensual and cooperative solutions that involve all main stakeholders. In doing so, we argue that while the three companies have followed similar strategic paths, their relationship to the Media Welfare State can be used to exemplify different approaches: Nokia is cited as an example of a *collaborative* approach, and Schibsted has followed an *adaptive* strategy, while the Modern Times Group is characterized by its *confrontational* tactic. The cases not only explain the development of these commercial enterprises, but also give insights into the nuances of the practical side of the public-private mix of Nordic media.

Chapter 6 contains a *summary and conclusion*. This chapter draws together the empirical findings of the studies of the book and discusses the solidity of the theoretical underpinnings of the concept of the Media Welfare State. The concluding discussion is organized around the key themes of the book. The studies show that the Nordic media systems develop and change, while maintaining key features, and the first part points to the strong elements of *continuity*, both in overarching principles and empirical realities. At the same time, Nordic media and communications are subject to *change*, as the forces of marketization, globalization, social fragmentation, and authoritarianism challenge institutions and policy regimes that in turn respond and adapt to them also in the digital age. The book applies a *Nordic* perspective—rather than studying each Nordic society as a separate entity—and this approach is evaluated and discussed. The last part of the conclusion critically discusses the assertion that there is a *crisis* in traditional media patterns and institutions.

// TWO //

Media Use

An enlightened public with equal access to information has been a key ideal of the Nordic welfare states. The citizens should not only be informed, but able and motivated to take an active part in both political and cultural activities. In a description of Nordic cultural policy aims, Duelund (2003, 488) states, "With the welfare state as a regulatory and mediatory player, citizens were to be educated as valuable, fully mature members of society with the ability to take responsibility for their lives on an individual as well as collective basis." Based on the same ideology, media policy was from the beginning conceived as a form of cultural policy, aiming to educate and inform the citizen and foster democratic participation (Syvertsen 2004).

The idea that the media are cultural institutions, important for the well-being and democratic participation of citizens, has tallied with a media user pattern characterized by commonality and egalitarianism. Although class differences do exist, people from all walks of life have enjoyed the same or similar media, and the degree of cultural and political polarization has been low. These features are vital to our understanding of the Nordic media systems as a type of Media Welfare State and illustrate how its organizational principles and historical features work "on the ground," so to speak. There is little use in applying elaborate policies and measures to media systems if these do not have consequences for the end user. Whether or not a media system is beneficial to citizens can, at least in part, be assessed by analyzing to what degree people have access to and use various media.

In the previous chapter, we identified four pillars of the Media Welfare State: universal services, editorial independence across the media spectrum, a cultural policy that extends to the media, and a tradition of cooperative and consensual policy-making. In this chapter, we discuss to what degree these principles have identifiable consequences for media use—both historically and in the digital age.

The chapter has five parts: Following the introduction, part 2 deals with the use of traditional media, and more specifically, how the Nordic tradition of high readership of print and factual media indicates a high degree of commonality and egalitarianism in user patterns. Part 3 discusses the access and penetration of new information and communication technologies and how the Nordic countries' evolvement into some of the worlds' most advanced information societies relates to the historical pillars of the Media Welfare State. Part 4 explores how Nordic populations use online media. We show that Nordic populations are above average on three types of uses: reading news, purchasing goods and services, and social networking. Part 5 discusses future prospects of media use. Here, we ask to what extent features often presented as challenges to the Nordic model, such as social fragmentation, immigration, and the rise of an elderly population, impact on Nordic user patterns. Part 6 summarizes the main findings.

In the chapter we compare the Nordic countries with other countries and regions in terms of media access and use. We base the comparisons on available statistical compilations, which have limitations: they do not always include all the Nordic countries, they are not always updated, and they vary as to which other countries and regions they include (see chap. 1). We try to clarify as we go along; in some sections we compare the Nordic countries mainly with other European countries; in other instances we use global statistics. Despite these shortcomings, we aim to show that the comparative homogeneity, wealth, and egalitarian social structure of the Nordic countries, as well as the homology of their media systems, lead to similar and distinct media user patterns. At the same time it is important not to overstate the case, as the Nordic countries belong to a larger group of societies in which individuals use media extensively and with great sophistication. When we speak of what is "typically Nordic," we speak of degrees rather than fundamental differences.

Use of Traditional Media in the Nordic Countries

The Nordic publics have been well informed and well integrated, displaying comparatively high interest and activity in both the political and cultural spheres (Thorsen 2011). These user patterns reflect characteristics of the Nordic Model and the accompanying principles of the Media Welfare State. The foundations of the Nordic Model and the welfare states can be traced back to the late 19th century, which was also the phase when the first universal communication services were set up. The decades immediately following World War II have been branded the "golden age" of the welfare state (see chap. 1). The media systems in this period were dominated by national and regional newspapers; highly regulated broadcasting systems; and publicly owned institutions in telecommunications, education, and culture, resulting in distinct media user patterns in each Nordic country. Despite the fact that media policy became more market-oriented from the 1980s onward, and that a range of new commercial services have been introduced, traits from this period are still strongly present in Nordic media use.

One distinct feature is that the Nordic populations have been keen readers of newspapers. In all Nordic countries, daily newspaper reading is the rule, and the proportion of people who never read newspapers is very low. This indicates a high interest in keeping up to date with current and political events, since even popular and tabloid newspapers continue to contain a comparatively high level of political and informational material (chap. 3). Finland tops the list of European countries regarding the frequency of reading newspapers, with readership figures high above the European average (Eurostat 2011, fig. 8.17). The five Nordic countries are among the top eight on Nordicom's (2010a) list of daily newspaper reach in selected countries: an overview that includes most European countries and the United States (table 6.17, 2008).

Parallel to the interest in public affairs, Nordic people have been high consumers of culture and are avid book readers; a large majority of the population regularly reads books as a leisure activity (Eurostat 2011, figs. 8.12, 8.16, for Finland and Sweden). The percentage of the population that goes to the cinema is also high in the Nordic countries, and, except in Finland, there is a relatively high number of cinema screens in relation to the number of inhabitants (Eurostat 2011, figs. 8.1, 8.4, table 8.2). Although it is not counted as media use, it is worth adding that in a European context, Nordic populations are very frequent visitors to cultural sites and frequently attend live performances (Eurostat 2011, figs. 8.7, 8.10). In the same way as newspaper reading is associated with the political public sphere, these features are linked with the cultural public sphere and a strong and egalitarian cultural policy, which also include relatively high public spending on culture (Duelund 2003, 488).

In contrast to the high figures for print and cultural media, television viewing is comparatively low in the Nordic countries. Europeans watch less television than North Americans, and also less than most people in Asia and the Middle East, with four of the five Nordic countries on the lower end of the European scale. Average household viewing time is less than three hours a day in Norway, Sweden, and Finland, whereas Denmark shows a more typical European pattern with four hours a day (Nordicom 2010a, fig. 3.21).

While Nordic people watch less television overall, the popularity of news and factual content on television has traditionally been high, as news has historically been the most popular content on Nordic television screens (Vaage 2012, table 33; Carlsson 2010b, 61). An important element of the cultural policy for the media is that television stations with public service privileges have been obliged to place news and current affairs centrally in the evening's schedule (see chap. 4). Since these channels have also commanded a large proportion of the national audience in prime time, the population in each Nordic country has by and large watched the same (or relatively similar) news broadcasts on a daily basis (Harrie 2010, table 20). The implication is a high degree of commonality and overlap where everyone has been informed about the same stories and events.

The picture emerging from comparative data is that the Nordic people are above average in terms of interest in informational and cultural content, and that the media have been perceived less as a vehicle for entertainment than in many other countries. In addition, Nordic user patterns regarding traditional media are distinctly egalitarian. On the whole, gender differences are small; for example, in contrast to most other European countries, Nordic women are just as avid newspaper readers as men (2007, figs. 8.12, 8.13; 2006, figs. 8.3, 8.9). Income and education levels do influence newspaper reading, but to a lesser degree than in other European countries (Eurostat 2011, figs. 8.18, 8.19). This is also true for television, where news viewing does not vary very much according to occupational or educational level (Vaage 2012, table 33; Carlsson 2010b, 61).

The use of traditional media and the popularity of a certain kind of media content in the Nordic countries reflect the principles of the Media Welfare State. The universalism of welfare state provisions is mirrored in a user pattern characterized by egalitarianism and commonality, and the cultural policy for the media has helped to place information and culture centrally in the population's media consumption. As we see in chapters 3 and 4, press and broadcasting content in the Nordic countries have also displayed less of the elite/mass distinction that by and large characterizes Western media. Later, we trace changes in user patterns; for the time being we point out that regarding traditional media there are strong elements of continuity in media use.

Digital Infrastructure: Internet and Broadband

Digitalization has brought momentous changes to the media landscape. There has been a proliferation of both traditional and new media, media content has migrated to new platforms, and a range of cross-media formats have come into existence. An unprecedented increase in the number and forms of devices for media use has also made it possible to enjoy media in new settings, at home and at work as well as on the go.

Behind these changes lies a process of convergence between telecommunications, broadcasting, and information technology, which since the 1980s have impacted on the agenda of policymakers, businesses, and citizens (Jenkins 2006; Lotz 2007; Storsul and Stuedahl 2007; Ludes 2008; Flew 2008). While convergence is often understood as a predominantly technology-driven process, Tryon (2009, 9) reminds us that media convergence "is also a deliberate effort to protect the interest of business entities, policy institutions and other groups." Convergence is used strategically and rhetorically to facilitate reforms and legitimate change (Fagerjord and Storsul 2007, 28; Storsul and Syvertsen 2007).

As digital markets mature, *convergence* is used as an umbrella term referring to "the new textual practices, branding and marketing strategies, industrial arrangements, and audiences behaviours enabled and propelled by the emergence of digital media" (Kackman et al. 2011, 1). The term *convergent media* refers to "content, industries, technologies and practices that are both digital and networked" (Meikle and Young 2012, 2). Parallel to convergence, there is a trend toward a divergence of information and communication technologies, devices, content, and formats. Systems and services increasingly overlap, although content and use have become more diversified (Storsul and Stuedahl 2007).

Comparative data indicate that the Nordic countries are among those that have most eagerly embraced convergence. By the turn of the first decade of the 21st century, three global surveys declared the Nordic populations as world leading in terms of broadband, Internet, and technological competence, as well as in investments and the use of communication technology (table 2).

Table 2.1 shows that Sweden is ranked as the world's most networked country, netting first place on two global indexes and second place on another. Sweden, Denmark, and Finland are among the top five countries on all three indexes, whereas Norway and Iceland also rank high.

The proportion of the population having access to the Internet is an important indicator of "network readiness" and the degree to which a country is

TABLE 2.1. The Rank of the Nordic Countries on Three Information Society Indexes: The Networked Readiness Index, Digital Economy Rankings, and ICT Development Index

Placement of Nordic Countries	The Networked Readiness Index Rank 2012:	Digital Economy Rankings Rank 2010:	ICT Development Index Rank 2011:
Sweden	No. 1	No. 1	No. 2
Denmark	No. 4	No. 2	No. 4
Finland	No. 3	No. 4	No. 5
Norway	No. 7	No. 6	No. 13
Iceland	No. 15	Not incl.	No. 3
No. of countries included	142 countries	70 countries	152 countries

Source: Networked Readiness Index data from World Economic Forum 2012; Digital Economy Rankings from Economist Intelligence Unit 2010; ICT Development Index from International Telecommunication Union 2012.

regarded as an advanced information society. In the Nordic countries, 9 out of 10 people use the Internet. Along with Luxembourg and the Netherlands, the Nordic population has the highest proportion of Internet users in Europe (Eurostat 2011, fig. 8.22; World Economic Forum 2012, fig. 6.02). Most Nordic households with an Internet connection also have broadband, although the capacity varies (Nordicom 2010a, figs. 1.16, 1.22). Moreover, broadband Internet has transformed social communication in education, health, and trade, and is essential for use of the Internet for social, creative, and communicative purposes (below).

Another key indicator is the dissemination of mobile phones. Again, Nordic users have been early adaptors. Practically every young and adult person in the Nordic countries owns a mobile telephone, and there has been a rapid dissemination of smartphones (TNS Gallup 2011). Mobile telephones are increasingly used as computers, changing the very understanding of what "computers" and "media" entails. Terry Flew (2008, 35) sums up the changes from the 1990s until the 2000s:

> While new media in the 1990s was largely associated with the internet, as accessed from computers, and for most people computers were boxy devices with screens that sat on desks, in the 2000s the range of digital devices that enable access to information and communication in ways that maximize speed and *mobility* has proliferated.

This coincides with the trend toward ubiquitous network connectivity and mobile broadband, which implies that consumers can always be online. In the Nordic countries there has been a rapid take-up of mobile broadband, thus indicating that consumers have gotten used to having access to advanced Internet services everywhere (Post- og teletilsynet 2009).

Why have the Nordic populations embraced and exploited convergence? And how has the region moved to a position of distinction regarding the penetration and use of information technology? Some of the elements that we have identified as constituting the Media Welfare State provide important explanatory factors: high public investment in infrastructure, high educational and skill levels, open economies, a business-friendly climate, and a commitment to universality and consensual solutions. For example, Nordic policymakers have seen broadband as crucial to economic and social progress, and have made a considerable amount of investments (e.g., Post-og teletilsynet 2010, 41–42). In our discussion of the Nordic Model (chap. 1), we referred to the historically strong state influence, whereby the state played a part as both a proprietor and operator of the communication infrastructure. In recent decades, this role has changed with the overall liberalization and marketization of communication, and the state has become less of a proprietor and more of a regulator. Although the role of the state has changed, the overarching policy goal of high quality universal services remains the same, and regulatory authorities play an important part in securing efficient services and defining minimum standards for consumers (Skogerbø and Storsul 2003).

Such minimum standards have in many instances been set higher in the Nordic countries than elsewhere. In her comparison between Irish, Danish, and Norwegian telecommunication policy after the liberalization in the 1990s, Tanja Storsul shows that the two Nordic countries—in tune with their "welfare state legacies and political cultures"—chose a broader scope for their universal service requirements (2008, 203). While universal service obligations elsewhere in Europe were predominantly focused on securing access to traditional (landline) telephones, Storsul shows that Denmark and Norway also made provisions to secure universal access to digital networks (2008, 210).

Policies to secure universal access to advanced, and not just basic, services are a defining element of the Nordic Model. In 2009, Finland made headlines as it became the first country in the world to make high-speed Internet a basic human right. In addition to investing heavily in broadband coverage, Finland's regulatory authority mandated a law obliging 26 operators to provide universal access in their area. Enshrining Internet access into law is a new type of policy measure, and illustrates how the principles we have identified as pillars of the Media Welfare State are updated and reaffirmed in the digital age (International Telecommunications Union 2011, 14; 2012, 149; Economist Intelligence Unit 2010, 8).

In a more generalized explanation of why the Nordic countries have encouraged and supported Internet and information technology, Ursula Maier-Rabler refers to the region's broader "information culture" (see chap. 1). In the socio-democratic culture that characterizes the Nordic countries, Maier-Rabler states that "access to information is a basic right and is seen as a condition for the public control of government" (2008, 58). This contrasts with the three other information cultures she identifies: Catholic-feudalistic, Protestant-enlightened, and socialist-centralistic. In contrast to countries with a Catholic-feudalistic tradition, for example, where there is no general right to acquire information, the information rights of the individual occupy the heart of regulatory provision in the socio-democratic system. Universal access to the Internet is a priority on par with access to information generally: "Because of their liberal tradition, Scandinavia has the most advanced constitutional framework delineating the free access to information," argues Maier-Rabler (2008, 58). In this sense, Maier-Rabler establishes a connection between the policy goal of universal access and the policies of editorial freedom and freedom of information that characterize the Nordic countries (see chaps. 1 and 3).

In our discussion of the Media Welfare State we also emphasized the preferences for cooperative and consensual solutions involving all main stakeholders, which is a continuing characteristic of Nordic communication policy in the digital age. In addition to policies to secure universal access, there has also been a shared commitment to actually use information and communication technology by all relevant stakeholders, including business, the state, and individuals. As stated by the World Economic Forum (2012, xiii):

> The Nordic countries are the most successful in the world at leveraging ICT. They have fully integrated ICT in their competitiveness strategies to boost innovation and ICT is present everywhere and in all areas of society, such as education and healthcare. (see also Economist Intelligence Unit 2010, 2)

Since the reregulation of telecom and media markets in the 1980s and 1990s, economic policy has been in the forefront of media policy-making, supplementing, and to some degree replacing, cultural policy goals (Syvertsen 2004). Digital infrastructure, broadband, internet, and mobile telephony are all market-led developments that have brought great changes to the media landscape. Yet, the discussion has shown that the commitments to universality and consensual and cooperative policies remain important in the Nordic countries and that these policy principles help to explain the countries' transformation to some of the world's most advanced information societies. In the next section, we turn back to the users and explore how they utilize the new opportunities.

Use of Online Media

People in the Nordic countries have extensive access to digital media. But how are these media used? In this part we discuss what kind of genres online users prefer and what type of activities they take part in. We use comparative statistics to see whether it is possible to discern a typical Nordic media user pattern, in the same way as has been done for traditional media. To provide a more in-depth portrayal of changing user patterns, we complement comparative data with case studies from individual countries.

The media have always provided opportunities for participation and feedback, but for most of its history, unidirectional transmission was the dominant mode. Since the mid-1990s and the emergence of digital media, the scope and significance of audience-generated content has increased (Jenkins 2006; Meikle and Young 2012). The second generation of Internet services, often referred to as Web 2.0, moves beyond simple forms of information and feedback, and extends the possibilities for using the web, both collectively and collaboratively (Mandiberg 2012; O'Reilly 2012). At the same time, traditional media, firms, and organizations have increasingly moved their activities online, linking up with social networks and providing opportunities for their customers to comment and respond. These moves are primarily motivated by needs to sustain customer loyalty and protect existing revenue bases, thereby illustrating the point that convergence is just as much about defending established interests as inventing something new (Maasø, Sundet, and Syvertsen 2007).

Since the Nordic countries have been among the first to achieve almost universal Internet access, the user patterns that have evolved are of great interest. The Nordic countries may almost be perceived as digital laboratories, providing a test case for studying how the possibilities of convergent media are exploited. Many have championed their liberating potential, as mid-1990s writers such as Nicholas Negroponte (1995), Howard Rheingold (1994), Sherry Turkle (1995), and Georg Gilder (1994) envisioned that digitalization would bring human liberation, a genuine public sphere, more fluid management of identity, and the overthrow of television. More recently, Yochai Benkler has argued that the information economy has shifted the balance from a market-based model toward an economy based on sharing and collaboration, thus improving conditions for individual freedom, political participation, a critical culture, and social justice (2006, 15). Lawrence Lessig campaigns for a greater openness of access to digital content, arguing that this will facilitate the move from a "Read-only" culture (RO) to a "Read-and-write" culture (RW). His concern is that culture should not only be consumed, but that people should "add to the culture they read by creating and re-creating the culture around them" (2008, 28).

To what degree do these aspirations reflect the emerging user patterns in the Nordic countries? Based on contributions such as those of Hyde et al. (2012), Mayfield (2006), and Schradie (2011), we can distinguish between different levels of online involvement and activity. On a basic level is the use of online media for obtaining information and consumption, requiring no input from users apart from making choices in the digital marketplace. On an intermediary level are various forms of sharing and showing (i.e., telling about one's experiences, views, or preferences, and communicating within one's own network). On a higher level is genuine collaboration and production, such as creating websites and blogs, creating and uploading digital content, and participating in collaborative wikis such as *Wikipedia*. This requires "an additional layer of coordination" that "aggregates the content into a new social object" (Hyde et al. 2012, 53–54).

Compared with other European citizens, Nordic users distinguish themselves particularly with regard to activities on the lower and intermediate level, such as consumption of online news, online shopping, and membership of social media networks. Comparatively, there is less interest in online activities that require more effort and involvement. In this part we also pay particular attention to blog writing and file sharing—activities that much fewer people take part in, but that are interesting because they show a strongly gendered user pattern: young women dominate the first, young men the second.

Online News

People in the Nordic countries are eager consumers of online news. In the same way as the Nordic populations have been devout readers of printed newspapers, Nordic citizens have followed their news providers as these have moved online. In 2010, one in three Europeans (34 percent) consulted online newspapers, whereas the proportion was 88 percent in Iceland, 78 percent in Norway, 74 percent in Finland, 63 percent in Denmark, and 54 percent in Sweden (Nordicom 2012a).

A high proportion of the Nordic populations also use the Internet for listening to web radio and watching web television (Nordicom 2012a). In all the Nordic countries, traditional newspapers and broadcasting organizations run several of the most popular national websites, only topped by Google, Facebook, and YouTube (Alexa 2012; Nordicom 2010a). This is yet another indication of how traditional media institutions remain popular and are highly trusted as news sources. Consumption of online news is a new activity, but also represents a form of continuity in relation to the strong tradition of the Nordic countries as typical newspaper countries (see chap. 3).

Online Purchases

Another area in which Nordic citizens distinguish themselves, with an above average level of activity compared with other regions and countries, is in terms of online purchases.

In the European context, Nordic citizens stand out with their extensive use of the Internet for banking and other commercial purposes, services that require high levels of access, competence, and social trust, as well as a high disposable income (Vaage 2011; Danmarks statistik 2011). The Nordic populations are competent and wealthy spenders in the digital marketplace. A Swedish study concluded in 2010 that "nearly everyone" in Sweden under the age of 55 used online shops (Findahl 2010a, 23), and 8 out of 10 also paid their bills online. Books, travels, and various cultural products were the items most frequently bought online (Findahl 2010a, 24). While every third European Internet user had purchased a cultural product in the last year (2009), closer to every second Norwegian and Dane had done so (Eurostat 2011, table 8.29).

Whereas commercial mainstream hits, major successes and bestsellers remain important in the digital marketplace, there has been an enormous increase in niche markets where "everything becomes available to everyone" (Anderson 2006, 11). The process has been described as a parallel trend toward disintermediation (a more direct relationship between creators and customers) and reintermediation (the emergence of new types of intermediaries) (Flew 2008, 201). Sites such as Amazon, eBay, and the Norwegian finn.no are prime examples, in which each buyer and seller does not trade much, but where a large number of sellers find a large number of buyers. In Norway, the buy-and-sell site finn.no, run by the established media newspaper publisher Schibsted, is the most popular national website, and such sites are also immensely popular in other Nordic countries (Alexa 2012).

Like online news reading, online purchasing is made possible by Internet and digital infrastructure. Online shopping is an increasingly globalized activity, where a few global operators constantly expand their operations, but there are also elements of continuity in the sense that some traditional media operators have developed new online business models.

Social Media

Thus far, we have discussed online activities that are on the lower end of the scale of involvement. Nordic citizens use online media in many ways as they would use traditional media; they read, as well as purchase goods and services. The third type of activity in which Nordic citizens distinguish themselves is on the intermediary level, as Nordic citizens are keen users of social media networking sites.

Facebook, generally available from 2006, has rapidly become the largest social media site, gaining a position alongside traditional media in popularity. Along with Google, Facebook is the most accessed website in all the Nordic countries (Alexa 2012). Norway, Sweden, Denmark, and Iceland all belong to (a rapidly growing) list of countries where half the population or more have a Facebook account (Social Bakers 2012). In all Nordic countries, the proportion that use the Internet to access social media lie considerably above the European average (Nordicom 2012a). Almost all Nordic youngsters regularly access social media; for example, among 16–19-year-old Danes, 92 percent had a social media profile in 2011 (Danmarks statistik 2011). Thus, Nordic populations have easily accepted social media and the dominance of a few global sites.

The explosive growth in social media has been crucial for driving up Internet use, and has changed media from one-way transmissions to vehicles of sharing personal information, staying connected with friends and family, and carrying out professional networking (Waters 2010; Meikle and Young 2012; boyd 2007; van Dijk 2006). A definite breakthrough for social media in politics came in 2008, when the Obama campaign effectively used them to build support and raise money (Hendricks and Denton 2010). Since then, social media has been obligatory in all political campaigns, including in the Nordic countries (Enli and Skogerbø, 2013; Moe and Larsson 2012a, 2012b).

Since social media involves so many people in so many different ways, it is difficult to generalize about the level of involvement and activity. On the one hand, there are indications that most people have a low level of involvement, predominantly browsing, consuming, or sharing limited pieces of information with their own network. For instance, Brandzæg shows that the majority of social network users in Norway are what he calls either "sporadic" or "lurkers," contributing little content of their own (2012, 11).

Other evidence indicates that social media may be transformative and powerful insofar as they extend the public sphere and constitute new forms of networked publics, extended in space and time (boyd 2007, 8). The communication among and within these publics may be trivial and superficial, but may also literally involve matters of life and death. One illustrative case of this is the enormous rise in the number of organ donors in Norway following a Facebook mobilization (Dagbladet 2010). In another exemplary case, Refslund and Sandvik (2013) analyze a Danish online memorial for dead children, studying the different phases of grief and the time it takes for parents to come to terms with a child's death. The ritual work around the site is complex and diverse, and the authors show how the site functions both as a place for individual mourning and as a basis for a community of sympathy and support.

A third poignant case is the use of social media in connection with the July 22, 2011, terrorist attack, in which a Norwegian man single-handedly assassinated a total of 77 people in Central Oslo and at the Norwegian Labor Party's summer camp for youth on Utøya. Facebook and Twitter were all used extensively both during and after the attack, as well as throughout the private, political, and legal processes that followed. Many of the youngsters at Utøya used social media as their primary way of communicating with the outside world; since many were in hiding, they were afraid to make phone calls, while still having a desperate need to communicate. Grydeland (2012, 142–46) shows how vital pieces of news first appeared on Twitter, such as the first news that someone was shooting at the camp, the information that many were dead and wounded, and the first identification of the perpetrator. A study carried out by the Norwegian public service broadcaster (NRK) shows that more than half the population in all age groups—including those over 60—perceived social media to be important or very important news sources during the attack. However, this study also shows that that an overwhelming majority was first informed about the attack by more established mass media, such as television, radio, or online news sites, and that these media were considered the most trustworthy by far (Tolonen 2011). Perhaps the most important uses of social media came afterwards, when not only Facebook, but other social media as well, were used to organize the so-called Rose Marches, bringing more than 100,000 Norwegians to the streets in a massive show of defiance and sympathy. A study shows that Facebook was the most important channel for informing those under 55 about these events (Enjolras, Steen-Johnsen, and Wollebæk 2012). Social media were also important in many other ways; for example, in propelling some pieces of music into the limelight as common songs of mourning for the entire nation (Maasø and Toldnes, 2014).

Blog Writing and File Sharing

News reading, online shopping, and social networking have become mainstream activities that involve a substantial majority of the population in each Nordic country. For our fourth and fifth points, we explore two forms of online use on the high and intermediate level of involvement: blog writing and file sharing. These activities involve a much smaller proportion of the population, and have turned out to be strongly gendered in the Nordic context.

Writing a blog, which is essentially a personal homepage in a diary format that contains observations, opinions, and recommendations, involves a high level of involvement and activity. What has turned blogs into a genuine social medium is the RSS technology, which allows readers to not just link to a page, but to subscribe to it, with a notification every time it is updated (O'Reilly 2012, 40). This technology is crucial for turning blogs into a dynamic form of communication, and is also the principle behind so-called microblogs such as Twitter. Blogs are highly diverse in their subject matter, but are similar in layout and share many of the same elements. In her book *Blogging*, Rettberg (2008, 20) identifies several subgenres, and singles out three types as being of particular importance: journalistic blogs, blogs as narratives, and commercial blogs.

Writing in 2008, Rettberg cites research that indicates that the distribution of female and male bloggers in the population is fairly even (2008, 155). Even so, Nordic survey data from recent years indicate that blogging is a strongly gendered activity. While there are not many bloggers in the population (6 percent of Swedes in 2010), blogging has become an integrated element of young women's online culture. Swedish research shows that it begins in the early teens; whereas in previous decades girls would have written a private journal, half are actively blogging as early as the age of 12. Furthermore, two-thirds of Swedish girls between the ages of 16 and 25 actively write or have written a blog (Findahl 2010a, 47).

Løvheim (2011), who has studied Swedish girl bloggers, argues that blogs play an important role in identity construction, and provide unique insight into the thoughts and ideas of a group that have previously primarily expressed themselves in private journals and conversations. Such "pink blogs," as they are called, are nevertheless met with disdain in the public debate. While most public attention focuses on blogs as a vehicle for political commentary, the overwhelming majority of blogs are used for personal self-expression or communicating about a special interest or hobby (Carlsson and Facht 2010, table 12.12). As a rule, the few blogs that have built a large enough audience to attract advertising income and exert influence in the Nordic countries are written by girls and young women in relation to fashion, beauty, and emotions.

In the same way as blogging has become part of young women's Internet culture, file sharing has become an integrated part of young men's Internet culture. The proportion of people who share files is not so high; in 2008, 11 percent of European Internet users engaged in peer-to-peer file sharing (Eurodata 2011; table 8.24, 2008). However, this type of activity attracts many young men, as Swedish data indicate that half of young Swedish men between the ages of 16 and 25 share files, and an additional 25 percent in the same age group have done so in the past (Findahl 2010a, 48). In Sweden, anti-copyright activism has also become a major political issue following the legal persecution of the Pirate Bay file-sharing site in 2009. After its founders were sentenced to prison and the payment of a huge fine, the Swedish Pirate Party won two seats in the European parliamentary election (IFPI 2011; see also Andersson 2009). Although file sharing is not very high up on the level of involvement, a commitment to file sharing may spill over into the political sphere.

Until recently, the film industry has been less affected by file sharing, though advances in compression and transmission technology have increased film piracy as well. Young men are also in this case the most avid actors; a Norwegian study shows that this group has a more liberal attitude toward file sharing than the rest of the population, but this is also the group that consumes the most films through regular cinema visits and DVD purchases (Econ 2008). The industry has fought file sharing on two fronts: by strengthening legal measures and encouraging the establishment of "cloud" services, of which Sweden's Spotify is one of the better-known music clouds. In all the

Nordic countries, record companies have partnered with Internet service providers and mobile operators (such as Telia, TDC, Nokia, and Telenor) to establish platforms in which customers can access music through computers or mobile devices (IFPI 2010). This reflects the Nordic principle of cooperation between the main stakeholders—namely, public and private companies and individual consumers.

The picture that emerges is that Nordic people are very active online, but that the activities that dominate place themselves toward the lower level of involvement. Compared with other European Internet users, Nordic consumers are well above average in their interest in news, consumption, and reading other people's expressions, but below average or average when it comes to being creative or expressing themselves. Nordic Internet users do not score particularly highly on posting messages or creating blogs, and with the exception of Iceland, the percentage of users who upload content they have created lies below the European average in all Nordic countries (Eurostat 2011, table 8.23, table 8.24). With their highly integrated and culturally homogenous populations, the Nordic countries are perhaps not where one would expect the most distinct outbursts of creativity or collaboration or the Internet. Still, it is interesting that in such resourceful populations so much of the online activity involves a continuation of traditional patterns, such as reading online news from trusted sources with roots in predigital society, banking, shopping, and the consumption of books and cultural products, and communicating and sharing information with one's own network.

Future Prospects for Media Use in the Nordic Countries

The last decades have seen a considerable fragmentation of media outlets. The number of television channels has significantly increased, traditional media have migrated to new platforms, and a plethora of digital services has been made available to the public. Historically, there has been a shift from spending on "big" and collective media to more individualized devices to communicate and receive content (Skogerbø and Syvertsen 2004, 53).

The fragmentation of outlets and services raises two important questions for societies in general and for the future of what we have termed the Media Welfare State in particular. The first question concerns the high degree of commonality and overlap in media use: to what degree does fragmentation undermine the common user patterns that form the basis of the argument about media as "social glue"? US writers such as Sunstein (2001) and Rosen (2004) are concerned that the fragmentation of media outlets will lead to a parallel fragmentation of media consumption, whereby people will only consume the media they agree with. They see a development toward "enclaves"

(Sunstein 2001, 77) and "egocasting" (Rosen 2004), which in turn will increase extremism and political polarization. Chris Anderson, the author of *The Long Tail* (2006), views fragmentation more positively: "Rather than being loosely connected with people thanks to superficial mass-cultural overlaps," he argues, digital media allows us "to be more strongly tied to just as many if not more people with a shared affinity for niche culture" (2006, 191). Still, in Anderson's universe, fragmentation is also inevitable, as "social glue" is giving way to "millions of microcultures" (2006, 183) and "thousands of cultural tribes of interest" (2006, 185).

The second question concerns digital divides. We have noted the historical egalitarianism of Nordic media user patterns, seen particularly in light of the fact that people from all walks of life, including both women and men, have had access to and broadly used the same media. It is contested whether new media have led to deeper information gaps or improved conditions for the have-nots. One view is that the divisions that characterized industrial society, including class differences, are no longer relevant, and that new technology provides more opportunities for all (Bell 1973; Negroponte 1995), whereas others claim that we are witnessing an increased digital divide, understood as "a gap wherein the wealthier, and the more educated . . . share in the global bounty to a greater extent than those with lesser economic means" (Davidson, Poor, and Williams 2009, 166). As Graham observes, "the sums invested under the banner of reducing the 'digital divide' are staggering" (2011, 214), but critics still argue that gaps increase. For example, Schradie (2011), who has studied digital production in the United States, concludes that the celebrated "digital commons" are dominated by elites, and that the overall pattern is one of "increasing digital gaps" (2011, 166).

As elsewhere, there is evidence in the Nordic countries that media user patterns are becoming more differentiated. We have already noted differences in the online behavior of young men and women. Here, we discuss three other potential dividing lines, socioeconomic status, immigration, and age, and also discuss to what degree differentiation implies social segmentation and digital gaps. The discussion in this part is based on case studies from individual countries, and the purpose is more in the line of identifying tendencies than of reaching firm conclusions regarding the whole of the Nordic region.

Socioeconomic Status

Nordic media use has been characterized by egalitarianism in the sense that people from all walks of life have consumed broadly the same media. Class differences do exist, but have been small compared to most other countries and regions. With digitalization, as well as increased globalization and marketization of the media landscape, there has been enormous growth in outlets and services. To what degree is there evidence for the view that information gaps based on education and economic status have become more pronounced in recent decades?

It is difficult to come up with conclusive evidence on this point. Existing studies indicate that socioeconomic status matters, but also show indications that gaps are levelled out. Skogerbø and Syvertsen (2004, 2008) investigated how households in different income brackets handle the costs of keeping abreast with the information society. They cite Norwegian data, showing that wealthier households spend more money on media and have access to a broader range of information and entertainment than less wealthy households. What they also demonstrate, however, is that all households, including those with low income, put a high priority on securing access to basic media and communication devices such as television, newspapers, mobile telephones, PCs, and the Internet (2008, 126–28). Although households with a low income have to use a higher proportion of their income on media than higher income households, there is little evidence of a fundamental digital divide. Due to lower prices and effective public policies to secure universal access, they conclude that "there is rather a tendency that some differences are levelled out" (2008, 128).

From a different perspective, Karlsen et al. (2009) studied social and economic stratification in television participation. The authors ask whether it is true that society is becoming more democratic since more people can participate in the media, and show that overall participation is very high; to the simple question "have you ever been on television?", more than a third of the Norwegian population—38 percent—responded positively in a representative survey (2009, 24). However, the roles that people are assigned on television are socially stratified; in roles involving a personal appearance, identification by name, and the right to speak, highly educated people are strongly overrepresented, whereas in the roles as extras in a television series or as members of a studio audience, more of a cross-section of the public can be found. Still, it appears that socioeconomic status is less important than age when it comes to explaining differences in participation. Younger people were much more likely to have been on television, to have applied to participate in a reality or lifestyle show, and to have responded to television programs in the form of voting or commenting (Karlsen et al. 2009).

Immigration

We have noted the historical homogeneity of the Nordic region, but these societies are also becoming more heterogeneous. Increased immigration and social pluralization lead to a further differentiation in user patterns. For instance, a Norwegian survey shows that inhabitants whose parents come from Asia, Africa, Latin America, or European countries outside the European Union are less prone to read newspapers and listen to radio than the population at large (Vaage 2009, 20). The same study shows that people with immigrant backgrounds are less interested in genres saturated with national references, such as television entertainment, and more interested in programs with global appeal, such as feature films. There is also less interest in national public service channels and more interest in international channels, commercial channels, and channels from other nationals and regions (Vaage 2009). Similar user patterns are found in other countries (Enli et al. 2010, 195; Paulsen 2010).

No doubt, many immigrants feel excluded by the way the national media address the audience, and they seek information and entertainment elsewhere. Yet, there is little evidence that user patterns are strongly segmented into different "enclaves" (Sunstein 2001) or "tribes" (Anderson 2006). Among both immigrants and the population at large, television and the Internet are by far the most used media (Vaage 2009, table 3.2). There is no evidence that immigrants only watch channels that reinforce traditional opinions and perspectives, as their interest in Norwegian commercial channels is equal to that of the overall population (2009, table 3.7). Additionally, immigrants also become more interested in public service television the longer they live in Norway (2009, 36). Immigrants use international media more, but also extensively use the media of their new homelands, which is a resource to learn social skills, gain information, and hear the national language (e.g., Paulsen 2010).

Also among immigrants, age is an important factor for explaining differences in media use. There is some evidence to indicate that media behavior among the young is more similar across nationalities and ethnicities than the media behavior of the more settled (Vaage 2009, tables 3.7, 3.8).

Age

Socioeconomic differences and migration account for some of the differentiation in media use, although it appears that age is more important. Young people increasingly depart from the user pattern of their parents and elders, and increased age differentiation seems to represent the most significant change in user patterns in recent decades. Although age differences in media use are not new, differences between people of different ages have grown. Young people watch more commercial television, use online media more, spend much more time on social networks, and are much less faithful toward traditional institutions than the older generations. For their part, older people strongly embody the historical characteristics of the Media Welfare State: They are more than averagely interested in print and information media, books, newspapers, journals, and magazines; they prefer the large and dominant television channels, particularly the public service television channels; and they are more than averagely interested in news, information, and current affairs programs (Vaage 2012).

Although the differences are profound, the old and young do not live on different planets media-wise. Teenagers and young adults remain keen users of traditional media, both in their offline and online versions (Carlsson 2010a, 12–13). Nonetheless, it is perhaps symbolic that the old and young have begun to behave differently toward what has traditionally been the most strongly uniting media element—namely, the watching of television evening news on one of the two main channels. While more than 80 percent of Norwegians 55 years and older saw television news on an average day in 2011, only every third person in their early 20s reported that they had done so (Vaage 2012, table 33).

The differences between the young and old are most prominent regarding digital media and communication devices. Table 2.2 shows the situation in Denmark, but also illustrates the overall Nordic pattern: the elderly use digital media less, and to the extent that someone is excluded from the information society, it is a proportion of the elderly population (see also Findahl 2010a, 53).

In all advanced information societies, there has been considerable concern that the elderly may be marginalized, and considerable efforts have gone into reducing this gap (Findahl 2010b; Danmarks statistik 2011). Although a proportion of the elderly are excluded, a growing proportion does use new information and communication technology. Another way of reading table 2.2 is by emphasizing the high proportion of retirees who actually use new media: every third person 65 and older uses the Internet daily and three out of four use a mobile telephone. As Findahl states in a study of elderly Swedish

TABLE 2.2. Use of ICT in the Danish Population: Retirees versus Rest of the Population, Percentages That Use Different Technologies

	Access to the Internet	Use the Internet Daily	Use the Internet to Read Newspapers, Journals, and Magazines	Use the Internet to Receive and Send E-mails	Use Mobile Phones	Use Neither the Internet nor Mobile Phones
16–64 years	93%	81%	67%	88%	97%	1%
65–89 years	49%	31%	28%	39%	74%	23%

Source: Danmarks Statistik 2011, figs. 63, 65, 69, 70, table 18.

media users, Internet usage among retirees is only commonplace in the Nordic countries and the United States; Internet use among the young is common all over the world (Findahl 2010a, 2010b).

Media as "Social Glue"

The case studies cited do not indicate that there is strong segmentation or a fundamental digital divide in the Nordic countries. Rather than a fragmentation into "enclaves" (Sunstein 2001) or "microcultures" (Anderson 2006), we see a tendency toward a more diverse use of media. This affects all social groups. For example, we see a development where different screens are used for different types of content. While shorter clips are often watched on the Internet, and movies and series are often watched on DVDs, broadcast television remains important for news, series, and current affairs (FICORA 2011). We further see an increase in parallel media use, in which people watch mainstream media (e.g., television) and use more segmented media (e.g., social networks) at the same time (Findahl 2010a). Rather than increasing fragmentation, it has been pointed out that social and online media function as vehicles for navigation, pointing people toward much of the same content, which continues to be "the stuff of water-cooler-conversations" (Webster and Ksiazek 2012, 52). Some of the differences we see are also life-phase related rather than related to socioeconomic or ethnic differences: while older people with much time on their hands watch more television, singles and couples without children under 45 drive up Internet use (Vaage 2012, table 39).

Our findings correspond with the observations made by Webster and Ksiazek (2012), who studied audience fragmentation in the United States. They conclude that to a high degree, the media continue to function as social glue and that the way users move across the media environment "does not seem to produce highly polarized audiences" (2012, 49). Rather than tribes or enclaves that do not intersect, they find "massively overlapping culture" (2012, 51). To a very small degree, audiences for different media are "composed of devoted loyalists" (2012, 40), thereby indicating little evidence of social polarization based on media segmentation.

We have seen that advanced forms of participation in both traditional and new media remain socially stratified and that some barriers to entry—material, technical, cultural, or skill-based—prevail. This is a general finding that tallies with observations from other countries (Graham 2011; Schradie 2011; Findahl 2010a). Nonetheless, there are also examples that barriers have been overcome if an activity is really important to someone. The example of young women is perhaps the most telling. In the early days of digital media there was a considerable amount of concern that women might be excluded, but, at least in the Nordic countries, young women have emerged as the most active group in terms of producing their own content on the Internet. As Findahl (2010a, 56) observes:

> Despite their noninterest in new technical equipment and difficulty in accessing computers in the initial development of the Internet, blocked by brothers and boyfriends, they now have their own laptops and generate their own content and their own blog culture.

In this part we have discussed whether the historical egalitarianism and commonality of Nordic media use may be undermined. Despite the differentiation of user patterns, we have not identified strong indications that digital gaps are increasing or that the historical commonality of Nordic audiences is being replaced by a fragmented universe of "millions of microcultures" (Anderson 2006, 183).

Summary

We started this chapter by examining the use of traditional media in the Nordic countries. We noted that distinct user patterns developed in the postwar years, the 1950s, 1960s, and 1970s, and that media were perceived more as a vehicle for information and culture and less as a vehicle for entertainment than in many other countries and regions. We also noted a high degree of egalitarianism and commonality in media use, corresponding with the ideals of universalism and equal access to high quality services that are central to the Nordic welfare states. We then focused on change, especially on how the Nordic countries have embraced convergence and new information technologies over the last few decades. Since the Nordic countries have been among the first to achieve almost universal Internet access, the user patterns that have evolved are of great interest. We have shown that the Nordic populations are above average in their interest in online news, online shopping, and social media, but, in a European context, less interested in the more active and collaborative opportunities offered by digitalization. In the last part we discussed media fragmentation and digital gaps, showing that although media user patterns are differentiating, there is little evidence to indicate that digital gaps are widening or that there is a fundamental segmentation or polarization.

In conclusion, we wish to highlight three issues.

The first concerns how the principles of the Media Welfare State are reflected in media use. In the same way as the Nordic welfare systems were set up to act as a social safety net, publicly owned and regulated communication infrastructures may be seen as cultural and informational safety nets. In line with the Nordic welfare state models these safety nets should not be seen as supplementary networks for the poor, but as high quality core services for the entire population and also as vehicles for active social transformation. The cultural policy for the media has helped to centrally place culture and information in the Nordic population's media diet, the commitment to universalism and the tradition of cooperative and consensual policy-making have secured nearly everyone access to state-of-the art information and communication services, and the liberal information culture and tradition of freedom of information have led to a focus on making the Internet universally available. Both social policies and communication policies have been characterized by the principles of universality, affordability, and diversity, and the principle that social and informational services should hold a high enough quality to serve everyone's basic needs.

The second issue concerns historical change—both within the Nordic Model and within the accompanying Media Welfare State. Just as the analysis of media systems helps us understand how the welfare state has been sustained and legitimated, the changes in media and user patterns help us to understand changes in the welfare state. In chapter 1, we showed how the Nordic Model and the Media Welfare State can be traced back to the late 19th century, and how the classic user patterns were established in the postwar years, the "golden era" of the welfare state. The Nordic media model—as well as the social model—was modified in the 1980s and 1990s, as commercial and private interests were awarded a more prominent role. Over the past decades, the Media Welfare State, as well as other elements of the Nordic Model, has been characterized by a private-public mix, in which the market plays a greater role and more services and products are on offer.

In this chapter, we have seen how some characteristics of media use change in this situation, while others continue. Commercial television and online services make up a much greater part of the population's media consumption, there is migration from print to online services, different type of media are used for different content, and global services like Facebook have achieved a popularity that equals that of traditional media. Yet, there are strong elements of continuity. There is still a high use of print and other traditional media, while the main television channels remain popular. Digital media are predominantly used for seeking information from trusted news sources, for buying services and goods, and for sharing information with one's own network.

The third issue concerns how media usage in the Nordic region distinguishes itself compared to other countries. We have pointed to the fact that the Nordic Model emerged from a series of comparative statistical analyses in the 1980s, and welfare state analysts have shown how the Nordic countries tend to create a cluster of their own along many dimensions. The same is true for indicators of media use that we have discussed in this chapter. Treating the Nordic countries as a single unit of investigation may mask national differences, which we have only noted in passing, such as Danes watching more television and Swedes reading less online news. Yet, as regarding both traditional and digital media use there are great similarities between the Nordic countries. These similarities become even more distinct in the digital era, where all the Nordic countries are identified in comparative surveys as being distinct and advanced information societies.

// THREE //

The Press

Historically, the printed press played a crucial role in the establishment of the Nordic countries as open, democratic societies. Within the newspaper sector there has been strong support for the view that the media should appeal to all and should inform and enlighten the population at large, and consumption of newspapers has been high in all social groups. However, both individual newspapers and the press as a whole are going through great shifts. In a time where there is frequent discussion of the crisis of traditional institutions, not least a crisis for print media such as newspapers, there is a need to reexamine the history, recent developments, and prospects of the Nordic press to understand its role in democratic society, and more specifically, in light of the discussion of the Media Welfare State.

The Nordic newspaper sector has historically reflected the principles of the Media Welfare State as identified in chapter 1. The Nordic countries stand out as early proponents of both universal literacy and universal communication systems, and the early institutionalization of postal services as public goods was vital to secure broad and equal access to newspapers. Institutionalized editorial freedom, the second pillar of the Media Welfare state, evolved early and distinctly in the Nordic press; indeed the long history of freedom from authoritarian and government interference is held out by observers as one of the more distinct features of Nordic publishing. The press has perhaps less than other media sectors been subject to extensive cultural and content regulation. Still, structural measures are instigated to positively influence media content and combat marketization, standardization, and globalization. Press subsidies, which arrived in the 1960s, are clearly a product of cultural policy, as the state intervened in a free-market structure to safeguard regional and political diversity.

The system of press subsidy, as well as other forms of support of privately owned media, is indicative of the fourth pillar of the Media Welfare State: the preference for policy solutions that are durable, consensual, and involve consultation between all main stakeholders. Although not every political party and media company agrees on all aspects of press policy, the level of conflict between and within parties and corporations is generally low. If conflicts erupt, processes of consultations are usually instigated in order to stabilize the situation and coordinate the interests of private and public media sectors. The raison d'être for this tradition, which remains strong, is that the press is seen as not just a business sector, but as a vital ingredient in democratic society, and that stable conditions benefit the press in carrying out this role.

With a basis in traditional institutions with long historical legacies, the Nordic press has taken on diverse market trends, faced economic shifts, and with various degrees of success embraced new technologies in the digital era. This chapter discusses the trends of globalization, marketization, and fragmentation, as well as authoritarian tendencies, and how they impact on the traditional press structure and editorial principles. The Nordic newspaper industry has—as elsewhere—been affected by the global challenges related to the migration from print to online media, and, although there are broad similarities in how these challenges are handled all over the world, we argue that there is a strong element of continuity in the Nordic strategies.

This chapter has five parts. Following this introduction, part 2 traces the history of the press in the Nordic countries under four headings: press freedom, self-regulation, press support, and a diverse press structure. Part 3 focuses on two key cases that are emblematic for the transformation of the Nordic press in the 21st century; the emergence of free newspapers funded entirely with advertising and the growth of online news, which destabilizes a structure based on print. Part 4 discusses the recent and future challenges to the Nordic press in terms of globalization, marketization, fragmentation, and recent authoritarian tendencies and discusses whether the Nordic press is in a state of crisis. Part 5 summarizes the discussions and singles out three overarching observations.

The Press in the Nordic Countries

In this part the Nordic press is discussed under four headings: Press freedom, self-regulation, press support, and a diverse press structure. We aim to identify unifying traits across the region and features that distinguish the Nordic press in comparison with other countries and regions, but also differences between the Nordic countries. Crucial to the chapter is the belief that the press, which is essentially a private and commercial sector, is vital to what we have defined as the Media Welfare State. Indeed, one can argue that the structural features and ideological principles that came to characterize Nordic newspapers throughout the early phases of the industrial revolution and mass democracy represent foundational features without which there would be no distinct Nordic model.

Press Freedom

The Nordic countries tend to cluster at the top of rankings that attempt to measure and compare press freedom worldwide. Since the launch of Reporters Without Borders' World Press Freedom Index in 2002, Denmark, Finland, Iceland, and Norway have more or less taken turns at the top of the ranking. The 2010 index had all Nordic countries, barring Denmark, sharing the number one spot together with the Netherlands and Switzerland. The report pointed particularly to Iceland and Sweden, as these countries stand out through a unique level of protection for the media and a particularly favorable climate for the work of journalists. By comparison, the United States was number 20, the same as the previous year (Reporters Without Borders 2010), but plunged to number 47 in the 2012 report due to the arrest of journalists covering the Occupy Wall Street protests. In the meantime, the Nordic countries all stayed within the top 12, with Finland and Norway topping the list (Reporters Without Borders 2012). The same pattern is clear in the 2013 index, which lists the 5 Nordic countries among the top 10 (Reporters Without Borders 2013).

A 2011 report by Freedom House, an organization with historically close ties to the US centers of power, points out that the Nordic region in this regard contrasts the European Union countries in general, which have lost their leadership status with 14 of the members, including Italy, Romania, Greece, and Bulgaria, in the lower part of the ranking. The report attributes the Nordic countries with the "free" label with scores between 10 and 13, while by comparison, the United States scored 17 (Freedom House 2011).

Measuring freedom is no easy task. The indexes as well as the measures stem from the Western part of the world. As such, we should be aware of the risk of biases (e.g., Hallin and Mancini 2012a, 2012b). The first question posed in the survey behind Reporters Without Borders' report addresses the number of murdered, harassed, threatened, and physically violated journalists. Sadly, the safety and working conditions of journalists remain an issue in many parts of the world, and it is important to count and report violations. In general, censorship and government interferences are frequent in Asian-Caribbean countries such as China and Burma, in Cuba, as well as some Arab-Asian countries, and eastern European countries such as Russia, the Ukraine, and Turkey (Hallin and Mancini 2004; Blum 2005). The high level of press freedom in the Nordic region therefore stands in sharp contrast to the censorship and oppression in these countries.

Such statistics can be used to sort democratic societies with a functioning rule of law and low levels of corruption from those without such features. As explanations for the uniqueness of the Nordic press compared to, for example, the European Union and the United States, these factors have less value.

To understand differences among such cases, we need to look at press freedom historically.

The Nordic region is characterized by the early institutionalization of press freedom. In some cases, the Nordic countries were the first to implement laws and systems to protect the press—systems that were later launched in Europe and elsewhere in the world. The most prominent example of such legislation in the region is the Swedish law for free print. Launched in 1766, it is considered the world's oldest constitutional provision of freedom of expression, dating back more than 20 years prior to the French Declaration of Rights' (1789) famous ascription of press freedom. Across the Atlantic, the amendment to the US Constitution securing press freedom was not written until 1791 (e.g., Chapman 2005, 13).

Key figures in the Nordic countries at the time were indeed inspired by human rights and freedom of speech movements in France and the colonies that were to become the United States, although societal developments in England were also an inspiration. For instance, progressive and forward-looking Nordic editors imported the understanding of the press as "a fourth estate" (which could control the executive, legislature, and judiciary) from what they termed "lovely England" (Eide 2000; Raaum 2001, 25, authors' translation). In this way, continental European ideas of a "public opinion" that could be cultivated and communicated from the wider society toward those ruling the country, including thoughts and concepts that emerged during the 18th and 19th centuries, travelled north.

Even so, the origins of press freedom in the Nordic countries are related to a specific historical and political context in the region—namely, common democratic, legal, and cultural traditions. This similarity is not least related to the fact that the region has been more integrated geographically and politically than current maps indicate. For more than a century, the entire region was even united in a single monarchy: the Kalmar Union (1397–1523). When the union was broken up, Sweden continued its rule over what was to become Finland until 1808, whereas the future Norway remained under Danish control until 1814.

If we look at the institutionalization in the latter state, the most important laws of the Danish-Norwegian autocracy included a chapter on printed texts, and the laws of censorship even prescribed the death penalty for violating the prescriptions (Eide 2000). In this context of royal authorization, editorial content covering societal issues was rare. The forerunners to what we today call newspapers can be traced back to early modern society, even in the form of handwritten notes telling about major societal events (e.g., Eide 2010 for the Norwegian example). Yet, the rationale behind the first Nordic newspapers, emerging from the 1630s in Denmark and approximately 100 years later in Norway, were not primarily public debate. Rather, these publications, like early paper-like publications elsewhere, grew out of a commercial need for trade communication. The content was primarily advertisements and business information, with the production skills transferred from book publishing, while the newspaper style was learned by copying foreign examples, particularly publications from Germany and the Netherlands (Eide 2001, 1999; Picard 1988).

During the 18th century, however, newspapers aiming at contributing to public opinion emerged in the Nordic region. First came Sweden, following the 1766 freedom of the press legislation, and then Denmark (e.g., Gustafsson and Rydén 2010; Picard 1988). In 1814, the Norwegian Declaration of Freedom instigated a subdued blooming of newspapers, especially in the 1830-40s. Nevertheless, the emerging Norwegian press was short-lived, as the country failed to gain independence, but instead was simply transferred from the Danish rule to a new Swedish-Norwegian Union that lasted almost 100 years more, until 1905. Soon after the union between Sweden and Norway was formalized, the Swedish authorities took control of the Norwegian press (Raaum 2001). Similarly to Norway, Finland only gained independence (from Russia) in 1917. While the first Finnish newspaper came later than in Sweden and Denmark (1771), the Finnish press was growing in numbers and importance during the 19th century. The years leading up to and following independence, a period with not only thriving national cultural movements, but also social and political turmoil, was the heyday of political newspapers in Finland (Tommila and Salokangas 2000).

As such, and in accordance with international tendencies, the free press developed in close relation with national public spheres in the Nordic countries. Beyond this general point, the growth of a modern press in the region exhibited different paces and time frames, as the rural colonies of Norway, Finland, and Iceland lagged behind the centers of power in Sweden and Denmark. On the other hand, through shifting borders, the interconnections between the countries meant that the ideas that formed the region with regard to press developments were very much the same. As a result, the Nordic countries' public spheres have been closely intertwined. Therefore, the notions of press freedom and its significance resonate across the region.

Press freedom is grounded in negative policy. That is, a free press depends on legal and political setups that reject interference from state powers. The solid foundation of a long history of institutionalized press freedom—a freedom that is continuously being respected—is one key characteristic of the Nordic region (e.g., Hallin and Mancini 2004, 145). Identified as one of the pillars of the Media Welfare State from its inception with the printed press, the principle of editorial independence was later transferred to new media such as radio and television. For the press, however, the freedom goes hand in hand with another measure, that of institutionalized self-regulation.

Self-Regulation

Several of the now well-known and widely implemented measures and instruments to support press freedom originate from the Nordic region, including self-regulation such as media councils, the media ombudsman, and the editor as the guarantor of editorial independence (Picard 1988; Barland 2005). The Nordic media live by the self-regulation doctrine of "let the press correct the press" (Eide 2000, 1999), with the idea being that journalists themselves should agree on a set of rules that the entire profession is held accountable to. These rules are constituted in fairly detailed codes of conduct, which are concerned with issues of both privacy and correctness. For example, the Code of Ethics of the Norwegian Press includes a paragraph on the avoidance of a presumption of guilt in crime and court reporting. In all Nordic countries, codes of conducts are managed by independent media councils that deal with complaints from the general public who claim to be victims of unfair press coverage. The media council then decides if the complaint is justified or not, with a common self-imposed sanction for the publication in question being to publish the media council's statement.

The existence of a press or media council is not a purely Nordic thing; it is also found elsewhere, for example, in other parts of northern Europe. Yet, in comparative studies, the Nordic ones tend to come out as among the strongest and most efficient, as journalists respect and pay attention to them (Hallin and Mancini 2004, 172–73; Humphreys 1996). As with the negative policy that creates the basis for a free press, the self-regulatory measures only matter if those subject to them are giving them weight and credibility. Here, the Nordic countries stand out. The Swedish press council can even issue fines, and a study showed that the Finnish practice of publishing decisions in the journalists' union magazine does receive attention, with as many as 98 percent of journalists reporting that they read them at least occasionally (Heinonen 1998; Karppinen, Nieminen, and Markkanen 2011). By contrast, in other parts of Europe, some publishers tend to pay less attention to the press council, thereby clearly diminishing its authority (e.g., Humphreys 1996). By further comparison, the United Kingdom and the United States are not described by institutionalized self-regulation to the same extent. On the contrary, self-regulation in these countries is informal to a large degree, taking place "within particular news organizations and in the wider peer culture of journalism" (Hallin and Mancini 2004, 223). Consequently, the importance of formalized self-regulation in the day-to-day constitution of the press represents a second key feature in our case countries.

Press Support

The Media Welfare State rests on both negative and positive policy interventions, and the regulatory regime for the press includes both types. The positive policy interventions we have in mind are the press support schemes, and in order to better understand these schemes, we need to take a closer look at the more recent history of the region's press.

Along with the development of the Parliamentary system in the latter part of the 19th century, the Nordic press formed a so-called party press. In this system, newspapers were owned, staffed, and directed by a political party and its close affiliates (e.g., Høyer 2005). The party press was really a multiparty press, with different papers biased toward different political views and ideological directions. As such, it was a clear example of political parallelism in the media (Hallin and Mancini 2004). This is a trait found today for instance in southern Europe, with the typical example being Italy, where each of the public broadcaster RAI's channels is seen to represent different parties or political strands (e.g., D'Arma 2010). By comparison, such parallel relationships between the press and political parties were significantly less pronounced in the United States and the United Kingdom.

The Nordic Socialist press became an integral part of the party organization from its very beginning, with Social Democratic dailies in the capitals proving so successful, that by the end of the 19th century their profits subsidized the extension of the party press regionally. The links between political parties and editorial decision-making were closest in Norway, although the party press was also important in Denmark and Sweden. In the first decades of the 20th century, the most successful Labour Party newspaper, *Socialdemocraten*, became Denmark's largest by circulation (Høyer 2005, 77).

Party newspapers were still the dominant form around 1970, as political party dailies represented 92 percent of the total number of newspapers in Denmark in 1968, 57 percent in Finland in 1970, 69 percent in Norway in 1972, and 50 percent of dailies in Sweden in 1975 (Høyer 2005, 79; see Salokangas 1999, 95; NOU 1992, 38; SOU 1975, 79, 65). No exact year marks the end of this system, but as early as 1974, the leading broadsheet newspaper in Sweden, *Dagens Nyheter*, had declared itself independent from party affiliation (Høyer 2005). By 1995, only 30 percent of the Finnish language press in Finland (there is also a Swedish-language press in Finland) had formal ties to political parties (Salokangas 1999, 97). By the start of the 1990s, 39 percent of

Norwegian newspapers belonged to the political press, but by the end of that decade, only one newspaper declared a party attachment or commitment in its preamble (NOU 2000, 79). The party press dissolved through "a long and gradual, historical process, influenced both by internal and external factors" (Allern and Blach-Ørsten 2011, 96; also, e.g., Schultz 2007). Among the key conditions imposing this change were the introduction of television, an increased sense of professionalism among journalists, and the success of apolitical tabloids (e.g., Høyer, Hadenius, and Weibull 1975).

On an institutional level, then, the Nordic press is no longer a party press. Still, on the level of content, studies have found that parallelism remains (Allern and Blach-Ørsten 2011, 98ff.): in some cases, owners retain mission statements that explicitly state ideological and political orientation, while content analyses have shown how political partisanship remains strong in Scandinavian newspapers. Both the way a political issue is framed and the way a newspaper interprets or approaches it are affected by a news organization's political history and traditions (Allern and Blach-Ørsten 2011, 102).

As the formal ties with the party system faded on the institutional level, newspapers became more dependent on the market. As a result of intensified market competition, the Nordic newspaper sector faced a downturn around the mid-1960s (e.g., Tommila and Salokangas 2000; Jensen 1997, 244ff.). The decline particularly affected the local press, where advertisement concentration led to hard times for all but the leading newspapers. Many of the second-largest newspapers closed down, and few news ventures were launched. The deteriorating situation in the press soon became a political issue; some parties were concerned that the papers closest to their views would not survive, and the situation was seen to impair the ideal of a democratic press structure in which the entire population has access to, and benefits from, journalistic pluralism. Editors and journalistic staff alike shared these concerns, and when the government discussed the possibility of positive policy measures in the form of state support to prevent further "newspaper deaths," representatives from the press were involved. In the debate, opponents feared press subsidies might hamper press freedom. In spite of this critique, in 1969 the Norwegian government constructed a scheme to subsidize the smallest newspapers that were losing out to local competitors. Sweden, Finland, and Denmark followed the Norwegian example, and all implemented press subsidies in the late 1960s and early 1970s.

These subsidies may be perceived as a form of cultural policy regulation, which we have defined as one of the pillars of the Media Welfare State. The justification for supporting a private press with state money was to uphold diversity on two levels: diversity of political opinions and geographical diversity. In addition to countering the ongoing marketization of the newspaper sector, the aim was to counter regional and local fragmentation and help sustain vital communities. The result was not state-funded presses, but a system where an element of public funding was introduced to counter the standardizing effects of the market, without undermining press freedom and self-regulation.

With the aim to mitigate inequalities in opinion making and secure a diversity of views, all the Nordic parliaments instigated some form of politically defined subsidies for the print media, although the exact layouts differ somewhat. While Norway and Sweden offer direct support to selected newspapers, the representatives of the press, supported by a political majority, have rejected similar proposals in Denmark. In Finland, the majority of the subsidy has been channelled into reducing the cost of postal delivery (Herkman 2009, 77; also Tommila and Salokangas 2000, 212ff.). The schemes have also changed in the decades since their introduction. For instance, by 1992, nationwide newspapers with a distinct editorial profile—whether religious, political, or cultural—became eligible for press support under the Norwegian system (Østbye 1995). Meanwhile, the Finns saw substantial cuts to the level of subsidies in the 1990s, as since then, €13–14 million per year have been designated for press subsidies compared to €79 million in 1985 (Herkman 2009).

Nonetheless, 40 years after the implementation of press subsidies in the Nordic countries, the system remains an important part of media regulation regimes, as newspapers continue to receive a considerable amount of funding. In 2009, newspaper subsidies comprised 3 percent of total revenue in Sweden, 2 percent in Norway, 1 percent in Finland, and 3 percent in Denmark (Nordicom 2009). In 2011, the estimated amount of press subsidies provided by the Norwegian Government was approximately €45 million, while Swedish authorities supported the press with approximately €66 million in 2009. And although similar systems exist in several other European countries, in 2010, the Nordic countries, together with Austria, France, and the Netherlands, were found to have the most efficient system for publicly supported newspapers (Lund, Raeymaeckers, and Trappel 2011). The exemption from VAT, still in force for print newspapers in all the Nordic countries, yields much more: according to the Norwegian Department of Finance, the country's scheme was worth €225 million in 2010 (NOU 2010). However, VAT exemption or reduction, as also found in many other European countries, serves all newspapers alike and does not aim at supporting pluralism as such with direct funding. Crucially, the Nordic newspaper ecology still includes commercially run local papers, regional papers, and national papers, and particularly in Norway and Finland, the local press remains of key importance. The central position of local newspapers in these Nordic countries differs from most other countries, where national newspapers are the backbone of the sector.

A Diverse Structure with Universal Appeal

The Nordic countries stand out compared to other countries and regions with their diverse press structure with universal appeal and high levels of newspaper consumption. As we showed in the previous chapter, the numbers of copies of newspapers distributed to readers in the region is the highest in the world. The three Nordic countries Norway, Finland, and Sweden each have a newspaper penetration that is between four to five times higher than in the southern European countries Spain and Italy, and over seven times higher than in Greece or Portugal (Elvestad and Blekesaune 2008; see WAN 2005). In Norway, where almost all citizens read newspapers, being a nonreader could even cause a degree of stigma (Blekesaune, Elvestad, and Aalberge 2012). The strong position of the newspaper in the Nordic countries can in part be explained by the comparatively late introduction of broadcasting, and especially the late coming of commercial television. Newspapers early on established themselves as the primary channel for advertising, as well as the main provider of daily news for the population (Eide 1999).

The number of published titles clearly matters in this context, which in turn points back to the system of press support. However, there are differences here within the Nordic region.

Table 3.1 details the results of a comparison from 2006 (Weibull and Nilsson 2010, 46). It shows Norway, Finland, and Sweden as the three highest ranking in terms of newspaper copies per 1,000 inhabitants, all above the United Kingdom. Denmark and Iceland have lower numbers, but as

TABLE 3.1. Newspaper Copies per 1,000 Inhabitants and Newspapers Existing per 1 Million in the Nordic Countries Compared to Selected European Countries (2006)

Placement of Nordic Countries Compared to Selected European Countries	Newspaper Copies per 1,000 Inhabitants	Newspapers Existing per 1 Million Inhabitants
Norway	601	16.4
Finland	515	10.5
Sweden	466	10.0
Denmark	287	8.2
Iceland	198	9.7
United Kingdom	335	2.4
Spain	110	4.2
Italy	156	2.0

Source: Data from Weibull and Nilsson 2010.

shown, they still rank well above countries such as Spain and Italy. The table further shows how the number of existing papers per 1 million inhabitants follows a similar pattern: The same three countries are at the top of the list, here followed closely by Iceland and Sweden, all above 8. By contrast, the United Kingdom had 2.4, Spain 4.1, and Italy 2 papers per 1 million inhabitants. Although the Danes are not as eager newspaper readers as especially the Norwegians and Finns, the Nordic region stands out in unison regarding the broad range of different newspapers.

The high level of newspaper circulation in the Nordic countries is fuelled by a nationwide and universal distribution system. A typical trait is the high level of subscription and home delivery, as between 75 percent and 90 percent of the total newspapers and magazine sales derive from subscription. This stands in sharp contrast to, for example, the Spanish and Italian markets, where the majority of copies are sold over the counter, with only about 10 percent via subscription (Nordicom 2009). The high share of subscriptions in the Nordic countries is linked with the importance of home delivery to establish habits among users such as the morning coffee and newspaper reading. In turn, the preference for subscriptions is related to demographic factors, including a scattered population and probably also the cold winter weather, which makes home delivery preferable.

Circulation and distribution are important for the egalitarian structure of the Nordic press, but the characteristic is also visible in the journalism (Karppinen, Nieminen, and Markkanen 2011; Von Krogh and Nord 2011). Most of the national papers in the Nordic countries address the entire population with popular and rather spectacular front pages that focus on crime, celebrity culture, and political scandals. Yet, at the same time, the national papers emphasize serious journalism such as political and social reportage, foreign news, and cultural debate. This balance—a middle-of-the-road approach—between the tabloid and the serious is a characteristic feature of the Nordic newspaper, and it is partly a result of the press subsidy system and partly a result of the relatively small populations in the Nordic countries (e.g., Lund, Raeymaeckers, and Trappel 2011, 49). On the one hand, the subsidy system requires the papers to have a news profile and would exclude purely sensationalist newspapers. On the other hand, the national Nordic papers need to address the entire population and cannot afford to draw a separation between, for example, affluent and less affluent publics. In contrast to the United Kingdom, for example, there is not such a clear distinction between "popular papers" and "quality papers."

In their editorial profiles, the national press in the Nordic countries have indirectly sought to eliminate differences between sociocultural groups, instead supporting the idea of one universal public (Eide 1999). This universalism and egalitarianism, as well as the structural and political features that sustain and nurture it, is a key to understanding the historical role of the newspaper sector within the Nordic welfare states.

Free and Online Newspapers

Massive changes affect the press worldwide. Intensified marketization, global and transnational ownership, and social fragmentation deeply affect the newspaper industry in the Nordic countries and elsewhere. The biggest change is arguably connected with the transition from paid to free news, whether free print papers on the subway or news distributed electronically via the web or other platforms.

Free Newspapers

From the mid-1990s until about 2008, free daily newspapers grew as an international phenomenon. In Europe and the United States, total circulation increased 119 percent from 2004 to 2008, while in the years that followed, this growth halted. One survey counted 133 newspaper titles in 29 European countries in 2007, but by 2010 the numbers were down to 82 newspaper titles in 29 countries (Nordicom 2010a, 216). Up until that point, free dailies had made a dramatic impact on the Nordic press, but in quite different ways within the different countries.

One Swedish company was first, coming to dominate the Nordic free daily markets, and also leaving its mark on the phenomenon of free newspapers globally. In 1995, Modern Times Group (MTG), the media arm of investment firm Kinnevik, which was under the leadership of the controversial Jan Stenbeck (see chap. 5), launched a novel form of newspaper in Sweden's capital: *Metro* should be a free "down market tabloid" with local content, aimed at young and immigrant readers (Gustafsson and Rydén 2010, 323). From staffing via content to distribution, *Metro* was the antidote to the traditional Nordic press: produced in a cost-efficient and low-status basement venue, and with an advertisement department (approximately 30 salespersons) that was bigger than the journalistic department (about 20 writers); *Metro* presented reorganized media content from news agencies, and provided compact and unpretentious articles on the most prominent stories. Rather than building a foundation of costly distribution over large areas to subscribers' homes, the company struck a deal with Stockholm's Traffic Authority to acquire exclusive rights to distribution at subway entrances—in exchange for a full-page daily ad (Andersson 2000; Gustafsson and Rydén 2010, 323).

After four months, *Metro* was Stockholm's second largest newspaper (Andersson 2000, 309–10). The success in Stockholm, the capital of Sweden, was the basis for immediate economic profit and international expansion, and by 2000, *Metro* was established in other Swedish cities, throughout Europe, and in South America and the United States—from Newcastle in the United Kingdom and eight cities in the Netherlands alone, to Rome in Italy, and in Santiago (the capital of Chile), as well as in Philadelphia in the northeast United States. The growth was enormous. By 2000, the global circulation passed a million, while in 2009, *Metro* reached 19 million readers through 56 daily editions in 18 countries worldwide (Parmann 2010).

But one country is curiously absent from the lists of free dailies. Notwithstanding one ill-fated 1997 initiative in the capital region of Oslo that closed down after five years, Norway was without a free newspaper for quite a long time. The reluctance toward free daily newspapers is linked to the strong position of the paid-for press and the high circulation of daily paid newspapers (Parmann 2010). A second reason is the market power of the expansive media company Schibsted, which originated in Norway and is one of the largest media companies in the Nordic region (see chap. 5). Among others, Schibsted publishes Norway's largest tabloid newspaper, *VG*, as well as the dominant national broadsheet, *Aftenposten*, and has a dominant presence in the newspaper and online advertising market. By 2010, the former newspaper had an average daily circulation of more than 230,000 print copies, and the circulation of the latter newspaper's morning edition in the same year was approximately 240,000 (MedieNorge 2010). Schibsted actively worked to prevent the emergence of free newspapers. Third, more so than the other Nordic countries, Norway has a geographically dispersed population and high average labor wages, thereby making distribution of free newspapers a fairly costly affair. Still, by 2012, some local newcomers were successfully publishing free papers in mid-size Norwegian cities (Hagen 2012). Importantly, the major Norwegian media companies do not shy away from publishing or investing in free newspapers outside the Nordic region. Schibsted publishes free dailies in Spain and France (*20 Minutes*) and even bought a share of *Metro International* in 2008.

Again, there are varieties across the Nordic region. While Norway was "spared," *Metro* made a deep impact on the press in the other Nordic countries, which all saw domestic ventures into the world of free dailies. *Fréttablaðið* (The Newspaper) debuted in 2001, and grew to become Iceland's biggest newspaper. In parallel with the general international trend, the years up to 2008 were the prime time for free Icelandic dailies, with the country's third largest paper also being free (Nordicom 2009, 49). In Denmark and Finland, however, *Metro* directly challenged the established domestic press actors. Launching a Finnish version in 1999 and a Danish one two years later, *Metro* fought traditional publishers such as Sanoma (in Finland) and Berlingske (in Denmark). By 2008, *Metro* was the biggest free daily in both countries (Nordicom 2009, 49), thoroughly changing the Nordic press in the process. By 2011, while the print runs of free dailies were still high in Sweden, the peak seemed to have passed (e.g., Facht 2012).

Metro was perceived as the incarnation of a new informational capitalism and was controversial from the outset, as incumbents claimed that the newcomer destroyed the market for serious news journalism. Modern Times Group's radically different strategy—explicitly low cost, and with an aggressive advertising agenda—clearly altered both the overall journalistic landscape in the region, journalists' working conditions, and the advertising market. Incumbent for-pay newspapers were seriously challenged. Modern Times Group defended the publication by pinpointing how *Metro* represented a clear alternative to the traditional paid-for newspapers by primarily addressing new audience segments, turning teenagers, immigrants, and others who previously did not read papers into readers (e.g., Andersson 2000, 382).

Nonetheless, the invention was at odds with traditional journalistic ideals, such as the idea of the creative and investigative journalist. Free dailies also created turmoil among those who entrusted the national press with the key task of sustaining a primary arena for public debate. In sharp contrast to the image of the news reporter with a high professional journalistic integrity, some argued that the free papers were produced according to an industrial logic belonging to the category of "the news factory." In accordance with this, *Metro* entrepreneur Jan Stenbeck described Metro International as a global franchise, as "the newspaper version of McDonald's" (Andersson 2000, 310). Such bluntly provocative statements only strengthened the opposition against the paper and its owner. On the one hand, free dailies altered the advertising market and intensified the competition for readers, thus impairing the conditions for paid newspapers. On the other hand, there is no denying that papers such as *Metro* really did create a new market, not least by recruiting nonreaders among the young and immigrants (Gustafsson and Rydén 2010).

In a commercial international context, this way of producing newspapers signalled a transition for journalism. In the years that followed, readers got used to news as something that was abundant and free. And the question of how to fund journalism came to be front and center for the press, including in the Nordic region. As such, with its new production and distribution routines and new content, the free print dailies represented an omen, or a head start, for the online newspaper.

Online Newspapers

The emergence and rise of free dailies is an aspect of recent press history that is easy to ignore since it flies in the face of the dominant trend of the press from the last part of the 20th century. The Nordic print newspaper sector saw a 20 percent decline in circulation between 1997 and 2007 (Nordicom 2009), which was not at all exceptional internationally. The downturn had to do with new ways to distribute news electronically. The phenomenon of online news dates back to the early 1970s, when videotext technology enabled the distribution of information via telephone lines or cable to television sets or personal computers in the United Kingdom, and, from the mid-1970s, via the Minitel service in France. Throughout the 1980s, media and communications companies experimented with information services distributed via television sets, for example, the *Chicago Sun Times*' Key Calm and Knight Ridder Newspapers' Viewtron (Gunter 2003). Yet, the "killer application" for electronic news was the World Wide Web and its growth into a mainstream media platform starting in the mid-1990s. A simple periodization of this growth is to separate the early phase from the late, with the turn of the millennium and the so-called dot-com crash (a sudden global downturn in the inflated business of everything online) as the separator.

Hence, the years leading up to the turn of the millennium represented a first period of online news in the Nordic region. The initial experiments were more or less random, often carried out by individual enthusiasts within a newspaper, or in a more orderly sense by publications with a professional interest in technology issues (e.g., Falkenberg 2010, 248). In retrospect, key media events stand out as important levers. In the international arena, the death of Diana, Princess of Wales (in 1997) and the Clinton-Lewinsky affair in the United States (from 1998) demonstrated the power of the web when it came to not only speed, but also to depth and community building (Allan in Falkenberg 2010, 249). Similarly, when the Norwegian Internet service provider Oslonett published the results from the Lillehammer Winter Olympics in 1994, the effect was tremendous (Rasmussen 2006, 31).

This way of generating online traffic through media events, breaking news such as sports competitions, political scandals, or natural disasters remains a typical trait of the most popular online newspapers, including those in the Nordic region. In Denmark, a different type of external event led to a first leap for online news: a 1998 strike among those printing newspapers made journalists turn to the Internet to get their stories out. As a result, both the content and the outlets rose quickly (Falkenberg 2010, 249). At that time, in the late 1990s, some local and most nationwide print newspapers were present online (e.g., Rasmussen 2006, 40). But ambitions were far lower than what we have come to expect. As late as in 2000, less than 25 percent of Norwegian newspapers updated their website during the day (Ottosen et al. 2002). By 2010, 89 percent of Norwegian newspapers with some form of web presence offered online news (Høst 2011, 16).

Established offline actors dominated Nordic online news at this point in time, although some online-only news sites did emerge. When the Norwegian *Nettavisen*, launched in 1996, published news around the clock, the news profile was similar in comparison to print papers, having recruited key editorial staff members from established actors. *Nettavisen* operated as an independent editorial rebel, and the main business idea was to offer updated versions of news stories published elsewhere (Ottosen and Krumsvik 2008). This is in line with the first online newspapers in the other Nordic countries, such as in Finland, which recycled editorial material from printed papers and produced their online versions with a minimum of resources (Heinonen and Kinnunen 2005). Along with features such as unlimited space, continuous publication, and interactivity, this is one among the different characteristics of what has become known as online journalism (e.g., Karlson 2006; Engebretsen 2006). Nevertheless, these features should not make us blind to the aspects of electronic news that represent continuity rather than change.

In general, pure online outlets without a print "mother" were rare in the Nordic setting (e.g., Falkenberg 2010), as the rule was that those who provided offline news also took care of the online arena. Beyond initial experiments, the established Nordic press chose different strategies when approaching the web during this first period. Together with the publicly funded broadcasting institutions (see chap. 4), some companies were driving the development. In Finland, Alma Media, a broadcast and press company with a long traditions as a newspaper publisher, which owned a portfolio of regional and local papers, invested heavily in online innovation, set up a range of services, and also bought Internet start-ups in the years leading up to 2001. The burst of the so-called dot-com bubble had a major financial impact on the Internet sector, and also triggered organizational changes. Meanwhile, competing newspaper publisher Sanoma chose a more careful path, only starting real online expansion in 1999. And by the end of 2001, as the company saw signs that the bubble was bursting, management was able to scale back its new media activities (Lindholm 2010). Norwegian-based Schibsted has perhaps been the most successful among the large Nordic media companies in this regard, and has profited from generating online traffic, not least Schibsted's newspapers, Swedish *Aftonbladet* and Norwegian *VG*. These papers were also used as vehicles for new add-on services, including the business site E24, a collaboration between two Swedish and two Norwegian newspapers (*Svenska Dagbladet*, *Aftonbladet*, *Aftenposten*, and *VG*), dating services (such as *Møteplassen*) and a weight-loss service (*VG Slankeklubb*) (Nordicom 2009).

The years after the turn of the millennium and the dot-com crash, around 2001, mark the beginning of a second period of Nordic online news, characterized by stable, but slow growth. As we saw in the previous chapter, Internet penetration and use has been comparatively high across the region, providing fertile ground for the take-up of new services, including news. The breakthrough of online newspapers has been comparatively more prominent in the Nordic region than the rest of the world (Ottosen and Krumsvik 2008, 25), with online news steadily increasing their market share compared to print newspapers. In addition to the investments in building a universal infrastructure, which provided a rapidly growing customer base, a crucial reason for this speedy development was that established media companies, which had competence and resources to enter new markets, invested heavily in online newspaper publishing.

Figure 3.1 illustrates the rapid growth of online news, focusing on Norway's leading tabloid VG. By the end of 2008, the online version was proclaimed "the most read Norwegian newspaper ever," reaching nearly 1.5 million daily readers (among a citizenry of under 5 million). That was almost 100,000 more than its print "mother" achieved when its circulation peaked in 2002 (VG Nett 2009). By 2012, the online version had over 1.8 million readers, while the print has continued its decline and was even surpassed by the mobile platform, which had 775 000 readers. This signalled a wider trend on two levels: First, no one could any longer doubt the shift from print to electronic means of news distribution. Second, and more interestingly, established offline actors were dominating online news, and well-known structural features still mattered, as the number of new entrants remained low, and geography and scope still defined readership and distribution (e.g., Falkenberg 2010, on Denmark). Additionally, the shift from print to electronic means is not all encompassing, but first and foremost concerns national and international news. The still large population of local newspapers in the Nordic countries have not yet prioritized online news provision. Norwegian statistics remind us that a substantial part of the local newspapers still only use the web as a secondary channel for publication. At the beginning of the second decade of the 21st century, there remained papers that only produced a few online stories per week (Høst 2012). Adding to this impression, the number of new market entrants in the form of designated online news actors was consistently low across the Nordic region. In that sense, the traditional institutions of the Nordic press remain strong in the digital era.

Online news in the Nordic region continues to be characterized by continuity as the already established actors have expanded beyond the online news-

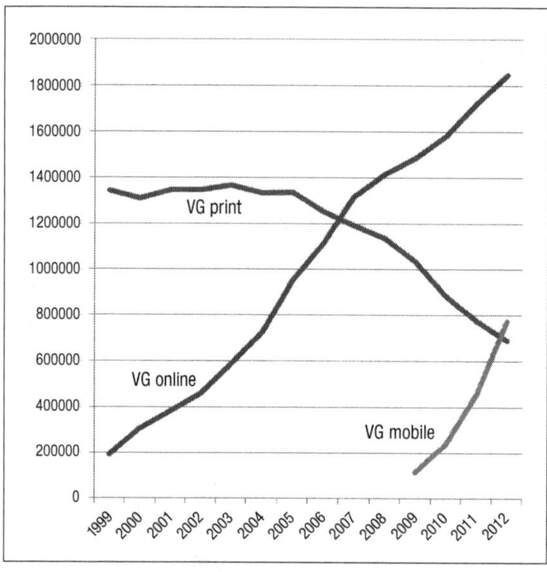

Fig. 3.1. Number of daily readers of *VG*, Norway's largest tabloid newspaper, on different media platforms. (Data from Medianorge 2013b: data for years 1999–2012.)

paper format. This expansion has taken two forms. On the one hand, online newspaper sites are becoming more interlinked with other web services, whether external or internal blog platforms, news aggregators, or different and changing social-networking sites. On the other hand, the news content itself has moved onto new platforms. The market for tablet computers, with Apple's iPad being the forerunner, is a case in point. By 2013, the major Nordic press actors all experimented with different iPad/tablet versions. Again, Norwegian Schibsted-owned *VG* serves to illustrate a wider trend. It had a total daily reach of 52 percent of the Norwegian population in 2010, which was spread over four distribution channels, of which online newspapers reached the most people (38 percent), while printed newspapers reached 23 percent. In addition, *VG* reached 5 percent of the population with their mobile phone news distribution and 4 percent through their own online community Nettby, which was soon to be overrun by Facebook and closed down (Fursæther and Møglestue 2010).

A decade into the 21st century, the electronic means of news distribution had reached a high level of sophistication in the Nordic countries. While the emergence of free dailies, spearheaded by Modern Times Group's *Metro*, had shocked the established publishers, by 2013, as news reading increasingly merged online via different terminals, the traditional news actors were still very much in the lead, although the game had changed.

Future Prospects for the Press in the Nordic Countries

It has become commonplace to talk about a crisis in the newspaper industry being linked to decreasing advertising revenues, lower circulation numbers, fewer readers, and reductions in staff. While studies have been conducted in various countries, the main reference point seems to be the US press. The crisis has not struck universally across the world, so it is not accurate to talk of a worldwide newspaper crisis (e.g., Benson 2010, 189).

To better understand the nuances in different contexts, historically aware, geographically comparative studies are needed (Siles and Boczkowski 2012, 12ff.). Moreover, the "rich and slippery" (Siles and Boczkowski 2012, 2) concept of a crisis might not fit everywhere. We argue for seeing the current and emerging changes of the Nordic press as another turn in a long history of recurring "crises" for the press: a turn that entails challenges as well as prospects. This perspective is in accordance with recent journalism research in the region, which frames the developments as "adjustments" or "reorientations" (Eide et al. 2012) or even approaches it through the study of innovations (e.g., Sundet 2012). Tracing the history of business news in Sweden, Denmark, Finland, and Norway, Kjær and Slaatta (2007) add to this impression that what we see are adjustments. While the concept of "crisis" indicates a retraction of serious forms of journalism, the authors show that this particular genre has expanded both in terms of journalistic status and quality and in the amount of resources allocated to it. As a case, the expansion of business news makes us aware of the continuing diversity of the press. Forms of content, economic models, or modes of communication emerge and fade over time, and we should be careful not to label the general development as a simple "crisis."

To take stock of the ways in which the Nordic press, and its role within the Media Welfare State, is changing in a digital era, we focus on three aspects: global challenges, the future of press support, and adjustments associated with increased participation by the public. In the early 21st century, these developments can illustrate how the overarching processes of globalization, marketization, authoritarianism, and fragmentation take new forms for the Nordic press.

Global Challenges

On a basic level, electronic news has not fundamentally changed freedom of the press in the Nordic countries. Journalists' privileges from the analogue era are transferred to the digital era, as the fundamental negative policy does not discriminate based on publication platform. However, this does not mean that the principles of freedom of the press are accepted and supported by all. As both societies and media systems become increasingly globalized, onslaughts on press freedom can come from anywhere at any time.

One illustration of the new situation is the so-called cartoon controversy. In this press debate, the ideal of freedom of speech was put to the test when the Danish print daily *Jyllands-Posten* published 12 cartoons of the Prophet Mohammed in a 2005 issue. According to Danish law, the cartoons were legal, and supporters of the decision to publish held the cartoons as a legitimate exercise of the right to free speech. The publication triggered protests against the paper (and also against Danes and Denmark more generally), and turned into a political crisis. Reactions were mixed in the Nordic press, and even though several editors sympathized with the Danish editor, they were generally reluctant to republish the cartoons because they wanted to avoid unnecessary provocation by publishing what many held to be blasphemous drawings (Stjernfelt 2009). In the end, newspapers in more than 50 countries reprinted the cartoons. Still, the Mohammed cartoon was first published in a Danish newspaper, which could be read as an illustration of the high standing of press freedom and liberal publishing policies in the press and among editors in the Nordic countries. More importantly, the case shows how issues of freedom of the press no longer rest within nation states, but take on a global significance. As a consequence, challenges to press freedom could emerge from outside the jurisdiction of press laws—illustrating how the challenge of authoritarianism takes new forms in the digital age.

The global nature of the information and communication industry and infrastructure represents market changes on another level. Novel distribution channels such as smartphones and tablet computers represent new bottlenecks in the chain of news delivery. Or, to use a well-established metaphor from journalism research: those who control these new devices and their systems emerge as a new kind of gatekeeper. To date, the most prominent example is the power of global players such as Apple, with the risk of US media laws and regulations affecting the Nordic region because of the US ownership of Apple, as their iPad has become a popular platform for news distribution. Apple imposes editorial control by prohibiting content that promotes competing products or conflicts with the strict US decency rules.

Nordic publishers have already been in conflict with Apple, albeit over issues that might not directly affect the core of press freedom; for example, the editor of the Danish tabloid newspaper *Extra Bladet* protested against Apple's censorship of their topless "page 9" girls, characterizing the restriction as: "A historical violation of the Danish constitution for press freedom" (Kampanje 2010, authors' translation). It is important to remember that the "violation" follows from the opportunity explored by the Nordic press for reaching new market segments via new distribution platforms—in this case the iPad. Apple is neither intruding on the press' established medium nor obstructing web expansion, as the potential and problem come as a pair. Nonetheless, the transformation is real and pertains to the press globally, and not just in the Nordic region. Yet, because of its early adoption of new media, coupled with its comparatively small and shielded markets, the emergence of the new gatekeepers could be seen as particularly challenging for the Nordic press.

The Future of Press Support

A key feature of the Media Welfare State is flexibility and adaptability; while there is continuity regarding the overall principles or pillars, concrete policy measures are modified and changed in the face of new challenges. The positive policy of press support is a case in point. We have seen how this policy originated in the late 1960s as a response to an earlier "crisis" for newspapers, at a time when politicians feared for the press and its societal functions due to changed economic conditions. A result of the migration of newspaper reading from the print to the online environment is that the traditional income model based on advertising sales, in combination with subscriptions and copy sales, has been threatened. The development of online newspapers has changed the basic rules of publishing. While the online newspaper readership is relatively stable, at approximately 80 percent of the population on an average day, the average reading of print copies has declined from over 80 percent to about 70 percent, and importantly, the share of those who read online only is growing and is approximately 10 percent (Nordicom 2010a). There is thus a widespread fear of a new wave of "newspaper deaths."

One of the most prominent online trends is the decoupling of news from ads and the revenue that they bring. Combined with decreasing profit margins following a global financial downturn, this constitutes a worsened economic situation for the press (Fenton 2011, 65). The search for new income models online is a global challenge that also affects the Nordic publishing markets, but perhaps to a lesser degree than most other regions of the world due to continued income from subscriptions sale and a growing online advertisement market, as well as the public support mechanisms of the national news production. In some cases, the global setbacks may not have stricken the Nordic region as hard as elsewhere. The region as a whole—and Norway in particular—has emerged fairly intact from the recent financial hard times. This again has resulted in a fairly aggressive innovation strategy in traditional media companies, such as in the Schibsted publishing house, which owns the dominant Norwegian classified online advertising website Finn.no (see chap. 5). On the one hand, this illustrates how traditional publishers manage to enter new markets online and maintain their position, while on the other, it is debatable as to whether the emergence of new commercial services more or less directly linked to editorial content should be understood as a digression from the journalistic calling or an innovative way to fund news reporting (Barland 2012). The economic challenges are also clearly real and important for the Nordic press (e.g., Nygren and Zuiderveld 2011, 145).

To supporters, press subsidies appear to be more important than ever as such measures are seen as the main vehicle to ensure diversity and combat social and political fragmentation, but they are also more controversial and harder to make fit. How and whether the subsidy system should be transferred from print to online media, and what guidelines and principles a new press support system should be based on, is not yet finalized. While a print market is easily divided, for instance, into regional, local, and national newspapers, online editions have a far more complex distribution and reach that are harder to measure. Around 2010, governments in the Nordic countries appointed committees to discuss and outline new rules for press subsidies in an online environment. Many of the suggestions were geared at sustaining the established press system by extending existing arrangements online, rather than abandoning print support for a brand new approach (e.g., NOU 2010). However, more radical suggestions have been raised, including the issue of public support for social media platforms (Christensen 2011, on Sweden). A related trend is that NGOs offer support to alternative media outlets or even individual bloggers, as has been the case in Norway (Fritt Ord 2010). At the same time, there are signs that some of the traditional support schemes are disappearing. In 2008, Finland changed its system for direct support of newspapers, so that the funds are now channelled through political parties (NOU 2010, 50).

Public Participation

The new technological possibilities online, specifically the ease with which more people can participate, constitute a third key development for the Nordic press. As with the fundamental negative rights of press freedom, the self-regulation system is also extended to new media and platforms. Mapping the ethical terrain of online news seems to be a task taken seriously by the press councils in the Nordic countries.

While the established Nordic press may have been fairly successful in moving online in terms of the number of readers, in general, the potential for changing journalism and news provision in the digital age into a more interactive model has only partially been fulfilled. Studies of the Nordic news operators' use of different tools that allow for feedback from readers, or other forms of interactive features, show a reluctance and merely modest successes (e.g., Finnemann and Thomasen 2005, on Denmark; Heinonen and Kinnunen 2005, on Finland; Engebretsen 2006, on Scandinavia). This state of affairs is not particular to the Nordic region, but also found elsewhere, both in Europe and the United States (e.g., Quandt 2008). The difficulties linked to creating a working model of interactive journalism have to do with internal organizational issues, economy, and editorial priorities. But the question of how to tackle the involvement of the users also touches on a number of ethical aspects that relate to the press's role in constituting a common public sphere.

In Norway, where space for anonymous commentary on mainstream online newspapers' articles has expanded significantly in recent years, the July 22, 2011, terrorist attack illuminated the ethical challenges, as the perpetrator cited a mixed bag of far-right extremist writers, bloggers, and organizations as his inspiration, claiming the end of democracy as a goal. Should such authoritarian views be debated in the mainstream media, or instead be silenced? Would it be better to try to moderate extreme expressions within popular and visible channels, rather than push them to obscure websites in the margins of a fragmented web sphere?

In the aftermath of the attacks, some media have imposed a stricter moderation and allowed less anonymity, but overall the changes have not been significant. In the longer run, striking the right balance on this issue remains a key challenge for the Nordic press and its self-regulatory regime.

Summary

The press has played a key role in the establishment and maintenance of the Nordic countries as open and democratic. We have argued that the historical role played by the press is essential to the establishment and development of the Media Welfare State. In this chapter, vital aspects are discussed under four headings: a well-respected freedom of the press; an established self-regulatory regime; state support for a private, commercial press; and a resulting diverse structure with universal appeal and high levels of consumption. The Nordic press has changed in the digital era, with the emergence of free and online news as key developments. In looking at the prospects for the Nordic press, and the ways in which its role within the Media Welfare State is shifting, we addressed the forces of globalization, marketization, authoritarianism, and social fragmentation. Summing up the chapter, we draw attention to three main points related to the peculiarities of the Nordic press structure.

First, we have seen how important features of the Nordic press continue in the digital age. In Finland, Sweden, and Norway, this is not least the case with the diversity in local and regional newspapers, which is important for the scattered population in at least two ways: (1) to secure public debate in smaller communities; (2) to reinforce local identity and settlement patterns. Newspapers help people feel attached to their local communities, providing a locally relevant source of information and space for debate—supplementing the national news arena sustained by the large newspapers. While, in the digital age, the Nordic press has explicitly met the same challenges as the press in other, comparable parts of the world, the ways in which these challenges are played out depend to a large degree on the previously well-established policy tools as a strong set of traditional stakeholders has ventured into the new world of, especially, online journalism. This speaks to the path dependence of media systems (e.g., Humphreys 2012)—the tendency that traditional institutions continue well-trodden paths in the face of new challenges.

A second point to draw attention to is the Nordic press as an experimental and innovative sector. The pioneering development of free print newspapers originating in the region, as well as the expansive commercial strategies of companies such as Norwegian Schibsted in the digital age, illustrates how the fundament of press freedom and well-respected self-regulatory arrangements serve as a platform. The Nordic press is not one united, internally defensive entity, but rather houses contradictory developments, not least visible in uncertain times.

This points toward a third observation. It might seem as if the building blocks of the Media Welfare State are unstable. For instance, it remains uncertain as to how and to what extent the Nordic press support schemes can be transferred to online media. However, such instability or uncertainty should not necessarily be read as an omen for the press in the region. We have shown how the specific tools used to sustain the Media Welfare State are being altered or even swapped for new ones as the Nordic Model adapts to new contexts. We can therefore conclude that the sector known as the print press is changing, but that there are strong signs of continuity regarding its role in the Media Welfare State.

// FOUR //

Public Service Broadcasting

The public service broadcasting corporations of the Nordic countries can in many ways be seen as cornerstones of the Media Welfare State. More than any other media structures, the public service broadcasters embody what we have identified as four key principles or pillars; they are publicly owned and universally available, they have institutionalized freedom from editorial interference, they are obliged to provide diversity and quality in media output, and their existence is based on broad political compromises and a high degree of legitimacy. Originally set up as radio monopolies during the interwar period, Nordic public service broadcasters have adapted and evolved, appearing today as self-confident, modern, and popular multimedia corporations.

The public service tradition in broadcasting is epitomized by the British Broadcasting Corporation, established in the mid-1920s. Together with the British and other northern European broadcasters, the Nordic institutions represent the stronghold of the public service tradition. In the northern European countries the public service broadcasters are generally well funded, have a comprehensive remit, and occupy a central position in society. This stands in contrast to more limited public service traditions found in eastern and southern Europe and in other Anglo-American countries such as Australia, New Zealand, and Canada, where the remit is less comprehensive, the funding more limited, and the position less central. Public service broadcasting in northern Europe contrasts sharply with the US public broadcasting system, which by comparison occupies a distinctly marginal position (Hallin and Manchini 2004; Hoffmann-Riem 1996; Humphreys 1996; McKinsey and Company 2004; Mendel 2000; Moe and Syvertsen 2009).

This chapter discusses how public service broadcasting relates to the Media Welfare State, focusing on the former monopolist institutions in each country. The chapter chronicles their origins as radio broadcasters and the later additions of television and Internet-based media. We show how public service broadcasting has faced a series of challenges (or "crises" as they are often termed in academic writing and debate), such as increased social pluralism from the 1970s, the onset of commercial competition from the 1980s, and the battery of changes associated with digitalization in the 1990s and 2000s. Although much of the literature and debate on public service broadcasting has a rather dystopic slant, focusing on whether public service broadcasting may survive at all in a globalized market environment, our specific analysis of Nordic broadcasters reveals organizations that have adapted well to changing circumstances.

In this chapter we point to the differences between the Nordic public service broadcasters, as well as to broad commonalities across the region, and compare the region's public service broadcasters with those particularly in other northern European countries and the United States. However, the research traditions within this field and the existing industry statistics pose limitations and certain methodological challenges for our Nordic approach: First, academic research on public service broadcasters in this region tends to have a national focus, and systematic comparative approaches are few. Second, while each country has comprehensive and updated statistics, data on the Nordic region does not necessarily include all the Nordic countries. Still, by carefully considering the available material we aim to show the shared traditions and functions of the Nordic public service broadcasting institutions in a nuanced way, although it is difficult to separate these functions clearly from those we find in other countries with a strong public service broadcasting tradition.

The chapter has five parts. Following this introduction, part 2 discusses the role of Nordic public service broadcasting in relation to the Media Welfare State under four headings: a uniquely central position, an equal and secure source of revenue, an adaptive approach to enlightenment, and authority as "the voice of the nation." Part 3 focuses on the transformation of Nordic public service broadcasting in the digital era through two key cases: the emergence of online services and the development of thematic children's television channels. Part 4 discusses the future prospects for public service broadcasting and argues that rather than being in a state of "crisis," public service broadcasters in the Nordic region are adaptive and remain popular. The final part summarizes the chapter and singles out three overarching points.

Public Service Broadcasting in the Nordic Countries

The concept of public service broadcasting first referred to the state-owned radio corporations set up in Europe in the 1920s and 1930s. Public service broadcasting has since been used to describe a variety of institutions, regulatory arrangements, social obligations, and types of programming. Common to all descriptions is that the concept refers to a form of broadcasting that is accountable to society, rather than to the state or the market. From the beginning, the purpose of public service broadcasting was "to provide a social utility rather than to maximize private profit" (Murdock and Golding 1977, 21; see also Garnham 1986; Scannell 1990; Raboy 1996; Syvertsen 1999; Born 2004; Moe and Syvertsen 2009).

All the Nordic countries have strong public service broadcasters with broadly similar characteristics. But since broadcasting structures are products of historical and political circumstances in each country, the specific organization and funding varies. Table 4.1 presents an overview.

The broad similarities visible in table 4.1 are due to common historical circumstances, but also reflect mutual learning and coordination. Like programs and content, regulatory models and examples travel from country to country (Smith 1998, 38). Nordic politicians and broadcasters have had extensive contact through common arenas such as the Nordic Council and the Nordvisjon, a cooperative broadcasting production organization. Today, the public service broadcasters in all Nordic countries continue to occupy a central position, receive substantial public funding, present a comprehensive and varied output, and maintain authority as *the* national broadcaster.

Centrality and Universality

The Nordic public service broadcasters stand out with their central position in their societies, and despite increased competition, no other commercial or publicly funded medium or cultural institution plays a similar role. Practically everybody uses their services, most on a daily basis. Recent audience research shows that more than 90 percent of the population tune in to the respective public service broadcasting services NRK (Norway), DR (Denmark), and SVT (Sweden) over the course of a week (DR 2012; NRK 2012; SVT 2012). Since its very inception and up until today, Nordic public service broadcasting's prominent position in society reflects what we have defined as the first pillar of the Media Welfare State: a universal and egalitarian structure where broadcasting is conceived as a public good. This central position needs to be understood in a historical perspective. The broadcasters originated as public radio monopolies in the interwar period. In the 1950s and 1960s, television was implemented into the existing monopoly structure for radio. Moreover, the central position is further due to the exceedingly limited output in the early decades. In Denmark, Norway, and Iceland there was only one national television channel available until the 1980s, and in Sweden and Finland only two (Flisen 2010). This situation contrasts sharply with television history in

TABLE 4.1. Overview of Public Service Broadcasting in the Nordic Countries

Denmark Original institution: • DR (Danmarks Radio)	1926: DR organized as publicly owned, license fee–funded monopoly radio broadcaster. 1954: DR starts regular television broadcasts. 1988: A second publicly owned broadcaster, TV2, funded in part with advertisements, commences broadcasts. DR is an independent state institution; TV2 is a state-owned limited company. From 2009, each of the two operators runs five TV channels, as well as radio and Internet services. DR is funded through a media license fee (€469 million in 2010). TV2 is funded by advertising and partly indirectly by the license fee (€57 in 2010).
Finland Original institution: • YLE (O.Y. Suomen Yleisradio/A.B. Finlands Rundradio)	1926: YLE established radio service. YLE never had a legal monopoly, and a commercial element was present from the beginning (de facto monopoly from 1934). 1956: Television first established as a private and commercially funded service, YLE later set up a license fee–funded service in companionship with the commercial service. 1964: YLE's monopoly restored when the public service broadcaster purchased its commercial competitor and used it to set up a second channel. 1987: A third channel set up as a joint private-public venture. 1993: The public and private structures separated. YLE is a state-owned limited company and runs four television channels, as well as radio and Internet services. YLE is funded through a YLE tax (€398 million in 2010).
Iceland Original institution: • RÚV (Ríkisútvarpið ohf)	1930: RÚV established as a state radio monopoly. 1966: Television began, funded with license fee and advertising. 1986: Commercial competitors set up. RÚV is a state-owned shareholding company and runs one national television channel. RÚV is funded through a media tax (€20 million in 2010) and advertising.
Norway Original institution: • NRK (Norsk rikskringkasting AS)	1933: NRK established as a radio monopoly. 1960: Television service officially opened. 1992: A nationwide commercial competitor, TV2, starts, with some public service obligations. The NRK is a state-owned limited company and runs three national television channels, as well as radio and Internet services. The NRK is funded through a broadcasting license fee (€570 million in 2010). TV2 is funded by advertising.
Sweden Original institution: • Radiotjänst, later renamed SR (Sveriges Radio AB)	1925: The Swedish radio monopoly held by an organization owned by the press and the radio industry. 1957: SR established, and ownership was more diversified, as several nongovernmental organizations were brought in. Regular television broadcasts.

TABLE 4.1.—*Continued*

	1969: A second television channel offered by SR. 1979: Sveriges Television (SVT) takes over the television services of SR as a newly constructed license fee–funded public service broadcaster. 1992: A nationwide commercial competitor to the public broadcaster, TV4, starts with some public service obligations. The current public television structure consists of three companies (SR, SVT, and the educational services of UR), all maintained by a state-owned foundation. SVT runs six television channels in addition to Internet services. The services are funded by a radio and television license fee (€684 million for SVT, SR, and UR together in 2010).

Source: Flisen 2010; Syvertsen and Skogerbø 1998; Bondebjerg and Bono 1996. All license fee figures from Nordicom 2012d, 34.

larger countries and countries with a tradition of commercial broadcasting, such as in the United Kingdom and the United States, where several networks competed from the 1950s.

The monopoly is often attributed to the technical limitation of broadcasting frequencies, although it was also seen as the best means to achieve universal service. As pointed out by Smith (1998, 39), the huge variation in the cost of transmitting signals in countries with different types of terrain is a "very important factor—still active in broadcast planning." The extension of broadcasting networks to the large and partly uninhabitable landmasses of Norway, Sweden, and Finland was costly and difficult, though the principle of cross-subsidy between central and densely populated areas was seen as crucial in achieving universal coverage. It was much easier to achieve universal coverage in the densely populated country of Denmark, not to mention countries further south such as the Netherlands and Belgium, where difficult geographical features were less of a rationale for the monopoly. However, in these countries, the monopoly was also more difficult to uphold, as the proliferation of cable networks led to a host of available channels, mostly from large neighboring countries like Germany and France from the 1970s (Brants and McQuail 1992, 160; De Bens 1992, 18–19).

The task of achieving universal coverage was taken very seriously in the Nordic countries, with the expansion in the 1960s, the first decade of television, being particularly intense. In Norway, the coverage increased from 35 percent of the population in 1960 to 95 percent in 1970 (Bastiansen and Syvertsen 1996, 132), while expansion was also rapid in Sweden (Kleberg 1996, 188), Finland (Hellman 1996, 99), and Denmark (Søndergaard 1996, 15).

The absence of competition, the small number of channels, and the universal coverage earned the corporations the description of "our most important cultural and political institution" (see, e.g., NOU 1972, 5, 25 for Norway). During "the golden age of the welfare states" (see chap. 1), the public service broadcasters set the national agenda, and anything they put out would become the topic of national conversation. Since the 1980s, however, technological, economic, and political changes have massively transformed the broadcasting context. Two waves of change can be identified: the upheavals and liberalization of the 1980s and the subsequent challenges associated with digitalization in the 1990s and 2000s.

Starting in the late 1970s, a series of social forces converged in a way that would eventually terminate the remaining broadcast monopolies in the region. Satellite and cable brought new channels, thereby undermining the technical rationale for having a monopoly, large enterprises lobbied for more liberal regulations in order to make a profit in the media and entertainment sectors, there was a pluralization of social movements and subcultures, and the "social-democratic era" was on the wane (Syvertsen 1992, 1997). Through its 1989 Television Without Frontiers Directive, the European Community decided to encourage transnational television, and all over Europe, new players began to challenge the position of the public broadcasters (McQuail and Siune 1986, 1998; Krebber 2002). Yet, it is interesting to note that in western Europe, Norway, Sweden, and Denmark were, along with Belgium, the countries that demonstrated "the longest and strongest resistance to commercial broadcasting" (Syvertsen and Skogerbø 1998, 224). It was not until the media arm of the expansive Swedish investment company Kinnevik beamed the first commercial Nordic satellite channel, TV3, into Norway, Sweden, and Denmark on New Year's Eve in 1987 (see chap. 5) that the national parliaments in the Nordic countries accepted commercial television. In Denmark, a second publicly owned broadcaster, which was funded in part by advertising, was set up in 1986, while in Norway and Sweden, private operators were granted distribution privileges in return for securing universal access and accepting some public service obligations (Syvertsen 2006, 40–41). As such, not only the public broadcasters, but also the private broadcasting structure, bore the hallmark of the Media Welfare State; they were compromise solutions allowing a measure of commercialization and advertising, but aiming at the same time to extend public service principles to the commercial sector.

The loss of monopoly implied a "dramatic dethronement" and an equally dramatic wake-up call for the incumbent broadcasting organizations (Syvertsen and Skogerbø 1998, 233; Bondebjerg and Bono 1996, 3). Whereas they had been slow to embrace competition in the 1980s, the institutions took a more proactive stand in the face of the challenges associated with digitalization. From the mid-1990s, public service broadcasters all over Europe lobbied policy makers to establish digital terrestrial television networks, fearful that they would otherwise be left without possibilities to expand (Levy 1999; Galperin 2004; McQuail and Siune 1998; Brown and Picard 2004). There was considerable doubt among politicians as to whether this was a future-oriented choice, but they were convinced by public service broadcasters arguing that the institutions would otherwise be marginalized and turned into "analogue museums" (Syvertsen 2008, 225). In the Nordic countries, but also elsewhere such as in the United Kingdom, the role assigned to the former monopolists' post-digitalization was rather that of "digital locomotives"; they were entrusted with the obligation to spearhead the transition to information societies and act as a bulwark against the threat of global media giants (Syvertsen 2008, 220; Aslama and Syvertsen 2007). This meant looser regulatory frameworks than, for example, their German sister organizations had to deal with (Moe 2009), further setting them apart from the state-owned broadcasters in southern European countries such as Spain, Italy, and Portugal (e.g., Brevini 2010).

From the late 1990s, public service institutions in the region played a key role in the building of a digital infrastructure in their respective countries. From 2007 in Sweden and Finland and 2009 in Norway and Denmark, the public service broadcasters made the switch over to digital television networks (e.g., Storsul and Sundet 2006; Brown and Picard 2004). Digitalization has made it possible for public service broadcasters to set up new channels, and their assigned role as digital locomotives has allowed them to enter new platforms, including the Internet and mobile telephony (Moe 2009). These moves have all been crucial for rebuilding a central position in the digital age. Indeed, as Søndergaard (2008, 43) argues, as a result of digitalization the public service broadcasters "have been strengthened to such an extent that hardly otherwise would have been possible." Furthermore, this shows how public service broadcasters have to a large degree retained their historical role in securing universal access to information and media content also in the digital era.

An Equal and Secure Source of Income

A further indication of the central role that the public service broadcasters continue to play in Nordic societies is the fact that they retain an equal and secure funding source. Up until recently, this funding across the region has been in the form of a traditional broadcasting license fee. In Iceland, the license fee was abolished in 2007 and the RÚV also takes advertising. In 2013, Finland introduced a specific YLE tax to be paid by everyone 18 or older, regardless of set ownership and media use (Ala-Fossi 2012). The remaining Nordic public service broadcasters, NRK, DR, and the three Swedish ones, all belong to a rare breed that have retained the license fee as the dominant form of revenue.

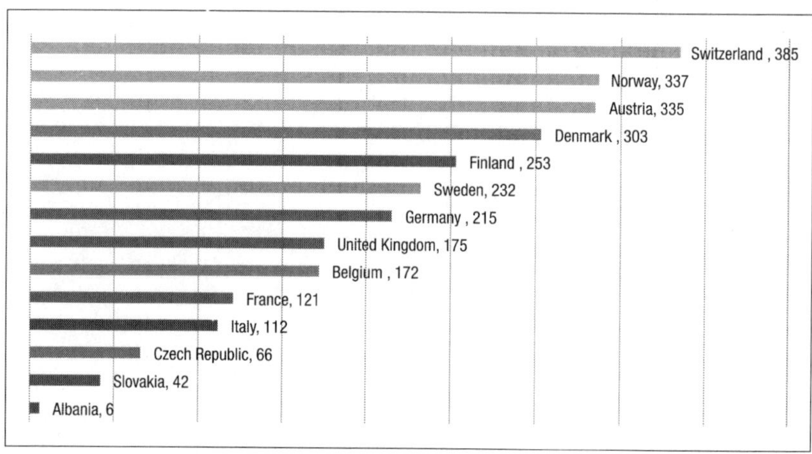

Fig. 4.1. License-fee levels in Euros in the Nordic countries and selected European countries 2010–11. (Data from *Wikipedia* 2012.)

In one case, the license fee has been extended, as in 2007 Denmark changed it to a media fee that covered all terminals capable of receiving audio-visual content—including personal computers and smartphones. More importantly, the four larger Nordic countries, Finland included, keep the broadcasting corporations comparatively well funded and free from regular radio and television advertising.

Figure 4.1 shows that the fees in the Nordic countries are comparatively high: Over €200 annually, and over €300 annually in Denmark and Norway. Such calculations are problematic, since they neither include VAT (which differs from 0 percent in Germany to 25 percent in Denmark), nor the numbers of nonpayers. Statistics from 2007 show that while license-fee evasion across the Nordic region was below 12 percent, many more ride for free elsewhere: In several European states, including Serbia and Italy, the numbers of evaders surpassed 35 percent (Berg and Lund 2012). Such differences clearly impact on the actual finances of public service broadcasting and also testify to the high degree of legitimacy and strong societal position of the Nordic institutions.

The license fee is a technical way of funding that has been closely linked from the beginning with the conception of broadcasting as a public good. In the same way that everybody was entitled to water, roads, electricity, and sewage, broadcasting was seen as a cultural and informational good that should be available to all. Since the cost to the individual consumer only depended on whether or not they had a television set, the scheme implied a massive cross-subsidy from those living in central areas to those living in sparsely populated areas and in the periphery, as well as from those who used the service less to those who used it more (e.g., the elderly and people with lower incomes). The principle of universality and affordability implied pressure on the government to keep the cost down, but as a universal service the fee was set high enough to provide comprehensive programming in all genres. In this sense, the change into media-neutral fees that also cover personal computer and smartphone ownership, or even specific taxes such as seen in Finland and Germany (Moe 2012b), should be seen as an extension of the traditional license fee.

However, the license fee also has another dimension, that of safeguarding editorial freedom, what we have termed the second pillar of the Media Welfare State. In principle, the license fee safeguards the autonomy of broadcasters from both market pressures and political pressures. Although public broadcasters pay increasing attention to popularity in the market, their financial return is only based on the number of set holders (close to the entire population) and not on the ratings of their programs or the demographics of their viewers. The license fee is also understood as a way of safeguarding the broadcasters from government pressure in controversial political questions; they should be self-funded rather than being forced to reflect the views of the government of the day (e.g., Moe and Mjøs 2013).

The continued existence of the fee in Sweden, Denmark, and Norway, along with the introduction of a universal and comprehensive funding scheme in Finland, testifies to the continued legitimacy of public service broadcasters and the commitment among key stakeholders to keep up both the funding level and the autonomous position of the broadcasters. In this case the stakeholders are the state, political parties, the government, and the license fee-paying population. The equal and secure funding has been discussed, but not attacked outright as in many other countries. The license fee has been retained in Britain, but has been severely criticized; for example, Margaret Thatcher, prime minister of the United Kingdom, 1979–90, allegedly saw the license fee as the symbol of "all that was wrong with British television and, indeed, with Britain more generally" (King 1998, 283–84). In the United States, public broadcasting has historically been starved of public funding (Smith 1998, 53). At the European level, there has been a recurring conflict between private and public service broadcasters over whether the license fee constitutes a form of illegal subsidy (Levy 1999; Mortensen 2005), and the license fee has in many countries—such as Cyprus, Portugal, Hungary, the Netherlands, and Belgium—been replaced with some form of taxation, in some cases leading to a reduced level of funding. While it is too early to evaluate the outcome of the recent Finnish changes, the Nordic approach nevertheless stands out as distinct: instead of undermining the prospects for public service funding in a new environment, the intention has been to create more "future proof" setups.

An Adaptive Approach to Enlightenment

From the early days of broadcasting, public service institutions were obliged to provide comprehensive programming, enlighten the public, and produce programs important to society rather than to individual consumers. As such, public service broadcasters stand out among the Nordic media; no other institutions have been subject to more extensive cultural policy obligations—defined as the third pillar of the Media Welfare State. Although the core of these obligations remains, the program output has been significantly modified in response to societal and media change. This adaptive approach to enlightenment, we argue, goes a long way toward explaining why Nordic public service broadcasters have maintained a central position in society. At the same time, the overall output on the channels in question continues to be different from that of commercial operators. This distinctiveness is crucial for legitimating both the public service structure and the equal and secure funding schemes.

To illustrate how the public service broadcasters interpret their obligations and remain distinctive in a post-digitalization television landscape, table 4.2 presents their program profiles along those of their competitors. The table is adapted from Ihlebæk et al.'s (2011, 229) study of prime-time programming on Norwegian television, and identifies five main types of channels, including the contribution of public service broadcasters.

Based on the overview provided in table 4.2, we can stress three features separating public service broadcasters in comparison with others. First, they have retained a broader mixture of genres on their main channels. In the early days of competition in the 1990s, all channels had a mixed-genre schedule, including commercial entertainment channels such as TV3, which provided news, sports, children's television, etc. (see chap. 5). Gradually, most other

TABLE 4.2. Nordic Television Channels Post-digitalization: Program Profile in Prime Time

Type of Channel	Program Profile
Thematic	Sports, news, children's, or other thematic content
Entertainment	Fiction, entertainment, reality, ads
Commercial; mixed	Entertainment, news, sports
Public service; mixed	Diverse programming with entertainment and sports, but also sizable amounts of information, culture, documentaries, and arts
Public service; in-depth	Music, culture, religion, news, documentaries, programming for minorities, special events, experimental programming, and only some entertainment and fiction

Source: Adapted from Ihlebæk et al. 2011 study of Norwegian television.

providers streamlined their output toward entertainment (reality, comedy, fiction) and directed their programming at younger and more commercially lucrative audiences (Ihlebæk et al. 2011, 233, on Norway). In contrast, public service broadcasters still target the entire population with their main outlets, labelled as public mixed channels in table 4.2.

Second, only the broadcasting institutions with some form of public privileges, whether traditional public service broadcasters or publicly regulated private television channels in the 1980s and 1990s, produce and transmit a significant range of factual genres such as news, current affairs, and documentaries (Ihlebæk et al. 2011, 230). This is programming that is important to people as active citizens, and not just as consumers.

Third, public service broadcasters are the only operators that use the extended channel space made possible by digitalization to significantly increase home-produced and externally produced in-depth programming, as well as experimental and innovative content (e.g., Bruun 2012). Together, this implies that public service broadcasting is crucial for retaining diverse and in-depth programming in prime time. If one or more commercial entertainment channels were removed, there would still be plenty of entertainment on Nordic television screens. If either the main channel or the in-depth channel of a national public service broadcaster went off air, however, the scope, quality, and diversity of the national television output would be dramatically reduced (Ihlebæk et al. 2011).

The mixed-genre schedule is a key feature of public service broadcasting and has been attributed great importance. "By placing political, religious, civic, cultural events and entertainment in a common domain, public life was equalized in a way that had never before been possible," argues Paddy Scannell (1989, 140). Taisto Hujanen (2004) claims that channels mixing information, entertainment, and culture are an essential feature of public service broadcasting and vital for broadcasting's ability to combat social and political fragmentation. Yet, the understanding of the mission to transmit "everything that is best in every human department of knowledge, endeavour and achievement," to quote the first director general of the BBC, John Reith (1924, 34), has changed over the course of history, and it was not even understood in the same way in every country to begin with. Scholars on British broadcasting have stressed how the British enlightenment ideal was somewhat top-down, based on the shared cultural assumptions of the aristocracy and the metropolitan bourgeoisie with their emphasis on art and high culture, and geared toward lifting the standards of the lower classes (Scannell and Cardiff 1991; Williams 1968). In contrast, the Nordic ideal was more universalistic, influenced by the ideals of the labor movement and the regionally based libertarian movements, and more geared toward the general evolvement of the human character (Syvertsen 1992, 95 for Norway). Skirbekk (1984, 306) argues that while the large European states developed a "non-popular tradition of enlightenment" and the United States developed a "non-enlightenment tradition of popularity," the Nordic countries developed a uniquely egalitarian tradition of popular education based on popular mass movements.

Yet, a paternalistic approach was evident also in the Nordic region to begin with. Kleberg describes the early task of Swedish television as the "general improvement of public taste" (1996, 189), and Bondebjerg refers to Danish television as being "influenced by a very strong informative and educational ideology" (1996, 41). Listeners and viewers were not always happy; Bastiansen shows how Norwegian viewers in the early days wrote letters to the country's public service broadcaster, NRK, complaining that programs were "too boring" and dominated by the tastes of the "cultivated" (1991, 40–46). From the 1960s, the influence of the traditional cultural and educational elites declined, and television everywhere brought more entertainment, new popular genres, and a more relaxed, informal communicative style (Scannell 1989; Dahl and Bastiansen 1999; Bondebjerg 1996). More profound changes came when the monopolies were lost and public broadcasters began competing with commercial channels. Studies from across the Nordic region show that public service broadcasters in the 1990s paid increased attention to ratings, introduced more entertainment and popular factual programming, and revamped their entire schedules based on scheduling principles imported from commercial companies. However, these techniques were not only used to maximize the overall number of viewers, but also to maximize audiences for domestic programming, information, and culture. Despite the massive changes in the 1980s and 1990s, comparative studies show that public service broadcasters remained distinctive in their program profiles, and continued to transmit considerably more factual, cultural, and in-depth programming than their competitors (Hellman and Sauri 1994, on Finland; Søndergaard 1994, on Denmark; Edin 2000, on Sweden; Syvertsen 1997; Ytreberg 2001, on Norway).

"The Voice of the Nation"

Nation-building has been a prime task for public service broadcasters everywhere, not least in the Nordic countries—catering to small populations spread across large territories. Not only did the broadcasters aim to connect the periphery to the center, they also emphasized the linking of the periphery to the periphery. In their role as the voice of the nation, the Nordic public service broadcasters set as their task to counter the standardizing influence of both globalization and marketization, upholding linguistic, cultural, and regional diversity and at the same time maintaing a common national public sphere. The aim was to tie the nation together; cf. Benedict Anderson's (1992) analysis of the role of communication in building an "imagined community."

Broadcasters' authority as the voice of the nation is expressed in various ways around the world, and has also changed throughout history. In the post-war era, Norwegian public service radio officially opened the program blocks by playing the national anthem (Bastiansen and Dahl 2008). Moreover, to serve their listeners with original music, the Nordic public service broadcasters established their own orchestras and took on a national responsibility of cultural patronage. The Nordic public service broadcasters still have orchestras, which are frequently used in programming, and perform at events such as the Nobel Peace Prize Concert and the Eurovision Song Contest, crucial ceremonies in the annual calendar of national celebrations.

In contemporary public service broadcasters in the Nordic region, but also in other countries, the voice of the nation ethos is communicated in news programming, media events, and in entertainment and drama. First, the weather forecast has traditionally been an important part of the news and information broadcasts in the Nordic countries, serving as useful information for fishermen and people living in harsh climate conditions, in addition to a symbolic gathering of the nation, as it "every morning drew the nation's map from north to south" (Löfgren 1990, on Sweden). Likewise, the main evening news broadcasts have addressed the national publics with an authority so convincing that watching was seen as a civic duty (Hagen 1992).

Nevertheless, the public has not always trusted the news from the public service broadcaster to the same degree; particularly in the 1960s, 1970s, and 1980s broadcasters were accused of both right- and left-wing biases, though all in all there were fewer clashes in the Nordic region than in many other countries (e.g., Britain). In part, this was due to the corporations' overall loyalty to the "social-democratic order" and their careful political journalism in the early days (Syvertsen 1992 for Norway; e.g., Lindt 1984), as well as being due in part to the more liberal tradition of freedom of information and a more open government (see chap. 3). From the 1960s onward, journalistic ideals and working practices became important elements of the rationale for public service broadcasting. This development had obvious advantages for the corporations, placing them even more firmly into the center of the nations' social and political stage. For instance, election nights and political debates became television events in their own rights, and the news and current affairs became flagship programs.

Public service broadcasting news continued to change as competition increased, not least in the direction of more infotainment, exemplified by more human interest, less foreign news, more crime and sport, and shorter news stories. In spite of these tendencies, several studies pinpoint prominent and continuing differences in content and style between commercial and public service broadcasters' television channels (Hjarvard 1999, 253–58). Although public service broadcasters have faced increased competition and a diminished status, there is still a high trust in Nordic public service broadcasters' news (e.g., NRK 2011).

A second aspect of the nation-building role concerns media events and the live broadcasting of history. These can, for example, be explored through the lens of Dayan and Katz (1994), who defined three different types of such media events: contests, conquests, and coronations. Contests such as the Olympics have traditionally been a type of sports event associated with public service broadcasters, serving as an arena for celebrating national victories. Even in the age of marketization and intensified competition, the Nordic public service broadcasters engage in the bidding for the costly sports rights. The archetypical example of a conquest is the moon landing in 1969, which was arguably the most celebrated broadcast of the monopoly age and served as a symbol of the authority of the national broadcaster to gather "everyone" in front of the sets (Bastiansen 1994). The subcategory of coronations can be exemplified by royal weddings (i.e., official manifestations of the status of the royal family as a national symbol). Even with competition from commercial channels, the public service broadcasters seem to have a hegemony on such events; for example, the wedding between the Norwegian crown prince Haakon Magnus and Mette-Marit in 2001 showed an 80 percent market share for NRK's broadcast of this event (NRK 2001). In Norway, the NRK covers the popular parades on the country's Independence Day, tracking the parades in different cities and small towns. In sum, this shows that public service broadcasters play a key role in communicating the nation's major, ritual celebrations, along with exceptional events and shocking catastrophes.

As a third factor, public service broadcasters in the region have built a nationwide television audience and communicated a national identity through weekend entertainment shows (Enli 2008; Bruun 2005) and domestic drama series (Gundersen 2005, on Norway and Denmark; Bondebjerg 1996, on Denmark; Höjier 1998, on Sweden). The adaptive approach to enlightenment implied that fiction and entertainment were also seen as important parts of the broadcasters remit, but that these programs were made to be different from typical commercial entertainment programs. From the early days of television, many of the entertainment formats came from abroad, but were transformed to suit the more serious entertainment profile of the Nordic public service broadcasters. For example, the early American television show *The $64,000 Question* was launched in Sweden, Denmark, and Norway (under the name *Kvitt eller Dobbelt*), with more academic questions and significantly lower monetary prizes (Enli et al. 2010, 110). The adaption of such programs was a forerunner of the current global format trade, where public service broadcasters also play a role (Enli 2008). More recently, comparative studies have shown that global reality television formats tend to be more down-to-earth when broadcast in the Nordic countries, a feature attributed not so much to cultural differences as to the dominant position of public service broadcasting within the television industry (Jensen 2007, on Denmark).

In some entertainment shows, public service broadcasters address the viewers not only as the voice of the nation, but also as a certain Nordic voice, such as for example in the television talk show *Skavlan* (SVT/NRK/DR), which is broadcast to a Norwegian, Swedish, and since 2013, Danish audience. In this hugely successful show, guests from various countries are mixed in a way that assumes that viewers are interested also in celebrities from other Nordic countries.

Fourth, perhaps even more explicitly than the entertainment shows, domestic drama productions thematize the history and culture of the nation. The historical drama series *Matador*, produced by DR in 1974 and aired a number of times in the Nordic region, is the most striking example. *Matador* portrays life across different classes in a provincial Danish town from the late 1920s until after World War II, gaining an emblematic status as a national icon by historically situating the plot in a context of crucial events in the country's history (Gundersen 2005, 201). Similar historical television dramas were made by other Nordic institutions, for example, the NRK's *Vestavind* (1994–95), which included "the national flag and waterfalls, fjords and mountains" in almost every episode (Gundersen 2005, 119). Using melodrama to tell the story of the nation, these series, in different ways, came to be key points of reference in national culture. Not least through such endeavors, television turned into a common subject for discussion and "a source for formulating [a national] identity and history" (Bondebjerg 1996, 42, on Denmark; e.g., Høјier 1998, 291, on Sweden). Over 20 years after the Danish television series *Matador* was first broadcast, in 2005, when the crown prince of Denmark announced his engagement to Australian Mary Donaldson, the couple was presented with a neatly wrapped DVD box of the television series at their press conference (Gundersen 2005, 201). The message is that *Matador* is—still—required viewing for any Dane, or a prerequisite for understanding Danish society.

The Nordic countries are small linguistic territories, and the broadcasters have traditionally imported a large share of the programming, particularly from the United Kingdom (e.g., Østbye 1982) but also from the United States. The effort to achieve a higher degree of Nordic production led broadcasters to set up a joint Nordic operation, Nordvision, in 1961, with the stated aim of "developing a common Nordic identity, (and) lowering the costs of television programming" (Hjarvard 1997, 47, authors' translation). Since then, Nordvision has not only survived, but also thrived. In 2010, it boasted a total of 4,000 coproductions and program exchanges, spanning all major television genres. The most prominent coproductions are children's drama series (Enli 2013) and Nordic crime series such as *The Killing* and *The Bridge*. Program exchange includes news and events; for example, DR and SVT sent a live news feed from the NRK for more than 24 hours in the aftermath of the July 22, 2011, terror attack in Norway (Nordvision 2012a). In addition, Nordvision has since its inception been a significant generator and distributor of factual television programming—a television genre with long historical traditions within the region (Mjøs 2011). Nordvision has therefore provided the Nordic public service broadcasters with unique access to a drama series and factual and news exchange, thus making their schedules diverge from that of their competitors.

Through both mundane everyday programming and extraordinary media events, and in both entertainment and information genres, public service broadcasters have built national identities and, to a degree, aimed to minimize social, cultural, and linguistic cleavages. This role has been criticized, both in the Nordic region and elsewhere. Stuart Hall, to name one central critic, argued that a united national public is in fact a construct and that public service could only survive if it adapted by "pluralising and diversifying its own interior worlds" (1992, 36). Yet, it appears that part of the success for the public service broadcasters in the Nordic countries goes back to their historical role in representing the nation and the ways in which this role is adapted, modified, and reaffirmed in the face of new challenges.

New Platforms and Niche Channels

Digitalization provided new ways to reach audiences, most prominently with the World Wide Web as a platform for all forms of media. Public service broadcasters in the region ventured onto the web as early as in the mid-1990s. They did so in a somewhat random and unorganized manner at first. Focusing on Swedish SR, Nord and Grusell (2012) describe how in the first phase leading up to 2000, the Internet was seen as something supplementing public service broadcasting at best, and within the institutions, management still discussed whether or not the web was something to strategically exploit (also Moe 2012, on Norway; Brügger 2012, on Denmark).

Around 2000, the web emerged as a truly mainstream media platform in the Nordic countries. In 1997, the share of the population with Internet access at home was 10–17 percent, with Sweden as the leader at 17 percent (Nordicom 2006). By the turn of the millennium, only Finland among the Nordic countries had yet to reach 50 percent coverage (Nordicom 2012c). At that point in time, all the Nordic public service broadcasters regarded the web as an important channel for communication with their audiences. The following years from 2000 saw a change in attitude within the institutions, as the web came to be viewed as something parallel to traditional broadcasting, and as something to be built more or less in addition to radio and television (Nord and Grusell 2012, 34; e.g., Erdal 2007, on Norway; Bechman 2010, on Denmark). Approaching 2010, however, a third phase was discernible, based on a perspective that seeks to integrate the web with traditional broadcasting (Nord and Grusell 2012; Moe 2009).

Online Activities

The strategic decision to integrate radio, television, and the web has led the Nordic public service broadcasters to develop a broad cross-media profile. The Nordic public service institutions distinguish themselves in this respect, not only compared to public service broadcasters in many other countries, but also compared to Nordic commercial television channels. Based on their positions as generally well-funded, universalistic, and adaptive institutions, aiming to retain their position in an increasingly Internet-dominated media universe, they have initiated activities on the web that are far removed from what they originally were set up to do. Here we discuss three types of online activities: redistribution of radio and television programs through the web, production of content exclusively for the institutions' websites, and ventures into external web sites.

Redistribution of radio, such as streaming or in the form of podcasts, was part of the public service broadcasters' web experiments since the mid-1990s. Television, however, required more bandwidth and was dependent on broadband services being more generally available (see chap. 2). Around 2005, Web TV was showing signs of maturity, most notably with the BBC's trial of their iPlayer, and public service broadcasters in the region followed suit. Launched in 2006, SVT Play offered all television programs to which the Swedish broadcaster is the rights holder for 30 days for free. Importantly, SVT Play is not only available through a stationary or laptop computer, but also on mobile devices. Hence, SVT Play is an example of the innovative redistribution of broadcasting content via new media platforms, with DR Radio App, a parallel service from the Danish broadcaster's radio division, being a similar example. In effect, such services bring the old institutions into the new media world, with their core activity remaining the same: the production and distribution of professionally made content to the wider public.

A second type of web content is that which is not broadcast in a traditional fashion, but made exclusively for the institutions' websites. From diverse but somewhat random collections of editorial content in the 1990s, the main websites of the Nordic public service broadcasters (yle.fi, sr.se, svt.se, dr.dk, nrk.no, and ruv.is) grew into sprawling sites encompassing a multitude of services. In addition to program-related information, sites typically include discussion forums, historical content, and text-based online news, much in the style of online newspapers. The public service broadcasters subsequently built portal sites that combined add-ons to individual programs and series, with exclusive content, including written items, that aligned them with newspapers that merged online. This is one feature that sets the traditional Nordic public service institutions apart from their commercial competitors (such as TV2 in Norway and TV4 in Sweden). The Nordic institutions clearly have more leeway than their sister institutions further south such as in Germany, where the public service broadcasters were not allowed to directly compete with the commercial press online (e.g., Moe 2009).

By 2011, the Nordic public service broadcasters' main websites were among the most popular and most visited in each of the countries: nrk.no (Norway), svt.se (Sweden), dr.dk (Denmark), yle.fi (Finland), and ruv.is (Iceland) are all among the top media websites in their respective countries (see table 4.3).

Nordic institutions also launched several more experimental services via their main websites, including "children's webs" (Nord and Grusell 2012; Enli and Staksrud 2013) and thematic subsites for youth. The Danish DR's youth services illustrate such an experimental approach; through a willingness to experiment with new forms and genres items were distributed on the web that challenged the traditional conception of what public service broadcasting was all about. Launched in 2000, DR's *Mujaffa* computer game is technically simple, with basic browser-based animation that is easy to learn. The avatar, Mujaffa, is a stereotypical young male immigrant, complete with broken Danish, and the game's task is to control his BMW through different parts of the country's capital, greeting friends, collecting gold chains, and picking up

TABLE 4.3. Top Nordic National Media Websites—2010 (weeks 34 and 41)

Country	PSB	Website	Ranking
Denmark	DR	www.dr.dk	7
Finland	YLE	www.yle.fi	5
Iceland	RÚV	www.ruv.is	6
Sweden	SVT	www.svt.se	11
Norway	NRK	www.nrk.no	6

Source: Adapted from Nordicom 2010b.

blonde girls. The game was launched in connection with a popular DR radio satire show incorporating the game's elements in a parody hip-hop tune. It was quickly criticized as racist and as confirming stereotypes and prejudices (Rasmussen 2003). Nonetheless, the game received generous praise not only through use, but also from commentators, who understood it as a "candid parody of attitudes toward immigrants delivered in an appealing package" (Egenfeldt-Nielsen 2003, 2). In a sense this is an indication that the public service broadcasters get away with more, due to their strong position and acceptance of their adaptive approach to enlightenment. But *Mujaffa* can also be seen to represent continuity in another fashion; it experiments with rhetorical tools akin to the Nordic public service tradition such as parody, satire, and irony. Though controversial, and with a debatable contribution to the overall public service remit, such endeavors make the websites of the Nordic public service broadcasters stand out compared to their European sister institutions (e.g., Moe 2009).

The third type of online activity is the public service broadcasters' venturing onto external sites. Strategically, the development of external content builds on an idea first voiced by the BBC—namely, that these institutions should be part of the web, and not just on it (e.g., Moe 2009). The services range from low-budget one-offs on platforms such as Second Life, an experiment with virtual worlds (Moe 2009), on the one end, to hugely successful sites on the other, such as the NRK's weather forecast site yr.no, which not only attracts massive user numbers in Norway, but also across Scandinavia and Europe and even in South Africa. The public service broadcasters SVT, YLE, and NRK also maintain their own channels on YouTube for the distribution of selected content (Moe 2009). Around 2005 the institutions also began to build profiles on social media sites such as Facebook and Twitter (e.g., Sundet 2012; Moe 2013). However, the incorporation of public service content into, for example, Facebook, did raise some concerns (Moe 2013) about the dilemma between employing new online channels and maintaining control as an independent provider of free media content on a commercial company's platform.

Compared to most other European public service broadcasters, public service broadcasters in the Nordic region have more generous leeway for expansion in the digital era. Their assigned role as "digital locomotives" (Syvertsen 2008) not only permits them, but also encourages them, to engage in online innovation on a scale that meets more reluctance in privately funded enterprises (Enli 2008). Their online production is intended to market their activities and strengthen their positions, but also to counter marketization and globalization through increasing the amount of genuinely regional web content.

Niche Television Channels

Digitalization not only imposed an expansion to new platforms, it also genuinely altered the context for traditional broadcasting platforms. The Nordic public service broadcasters responded to the massive expansion of commercial niche television channels by dramatically expanding their own channel portfolios.

In the years leading up to 2010, the Nordic public service broadcasters launched digitally distributed television channels catering to different niches. In line with the public service remit, the niche channels targeted interest groups and viewer segments traditionally associated with publicly funded institutions. Examples of the early niche television channels included a channel for education (SVT Kunskapskanalen, 2004), a television channel for news in Swedish for Finns (YLE's FST5, 2001), and a television channel for culture and history (DR K, 2009). Although niche television channels have been launched as additions to the public service broadcasters' main channels, the segmentation of media content and the targeting of certain parts of the television audience have been controversial as they represent a break from the traditional generalist television channels that cater to the whole population.

A particular interest among the Nordic public service broadcasters was to develop children's television channels, both because serving children as an audience segment had been an important obligation in the public service broadcasting tradition and because the Nordic executives realized that the competition from global niche channels such as the Disney Channel was a real threat to their hegemony in child-user segments (D'Arma, Enli, and Steemers 2010). Around the millennium, the Nordic broadcasters developed a plan to launch a Nordic children's channel in order to meet international competition with a Nordic collaborative project. However, the plan was never realized, partly because of linguistic, economic, and technological differences, though instead of one Nordic channel, separate national public service niche channels were launched. Sweden was the first Nordic country to launch a children's channel (Barnkanalen, 2003), followed by Norway (NRK Super, 2007), and Denmark (DR Ramasjang, 2009).

In contrast to the global content library circulated by commercial television channels for children, the Nordic public service channels produce and acquire programming from their respective countries with domestic presenters and participants, including a range of local dialects. The Norwegian television channel for children, NRK Super, even includes specific programming in the language of the Nordic region's indigenous Sami people. Approximately 25 percent of the total programming output of NRK Super is produced in Norway, reflecting cultural and linguistic diversity, and this type of content as a rule is broadcast in primetime. This means that a majority of programming, approximately 75 percent, is acquired from the international market, and dubbing is frequently used to appeal to Nordic children. Still, it is the domestic programming that spearheads NRK Super's operations, and the domestic drama productions are the channel's flagships (Enli 2013), in addition to the daily news program (*Supernytt*) for children aged 8–12, which has been rewarded with national and international prizes for serving children as citizens. NRK Super has also entered the merchandising market and offers a limited range of spin-off products based on the television channel's most popular domestically produced programming. As such, NRK Super also competes with the global commercial television channels' merchandising operations, and Disney's in particular (Mjøs 2010b)

The launch of children's television channels is a further indication of the public service broadcasters' adaptive approach to enlightenment: where the aim in the monopoly era was to activate kids to turn off television, the same institutions some decades later clearly contribute to the 24/7 cross-platform output of niche content that tempts children into watching. This adaption of the original remit is not only accepted, but applauded by policymakers and others as a necessary transformation of the original conception of public service broadcasting in an era where commercial and global enterprises constantly expand their output.

Future Prospects for Public Service Broadcasting in the Nordic Countries

Throughout their history, the public service broadcasters have been exceedingly important for politics and culture in the Nordic region, and they reflect the organizational principles of the Media Welfare State. We have shown that the institutions have been challenged on a number of occasions, but also that they have faced the challenges proactively and strenghtened their position on a number of counts. In this part, we discuss two questions that are crucial for public service broadcasting's future. These are the question of whether public service broadcasing is in crisis and the question of how the institutions will manage the transformation from public service broadcasting to public service media.

A Crisis for Public Service Broadcasting?

The future of public service broadcasting has greatly interested scholars, especially since around 1980, when most European public service broadcasters lost their monopoly position. The discussion of whether public service broadcasting is in a state of crisis, and what the outcome will be, is conducted on two levels: one normative and one empirical.

On the normative level, each new technological innovation brings forward new and old ideas about public service broadcasting being an anachronism (see Syvertsen 2008). With the advent of the digital age, cyberoptimists and others enthusiastic about new media forecasted the end of public service broadcasting and saw the Internet as a vehicle to facilitate a more direct dialogue among citizens (e.g., Coleman and Götze 2001; Froomkin 2004). The opposite normative position also surfaces with every technological advance; believers in public service broadcasting fervently argue that this construction is more important than ever and must be defended at all costs. These defenders point to ideal principles and very often to the need to sustain a public sphere with strong institutions independent of both the market and the state (see Moe 2009 for overview). In the digital age, there is widespread concern that the public sphere may fragment and that we may see a Balkanization of public discourse (Sunstein 2001; see also chap. 2). In this situation, the public services broadcasters, as key institutions of the Media Welfare State, are seen as crucial to draw everybody into a common discussion, at least on some occasions.

On the empirical level, the debate over whether public service broadcasting is in crisis is based on different interpretations of the impact of competition and commercialization. Critics argue that public service broadcasters are weak and vulnerable and unable to construct a proper defense against the onslaught of commercial forces (see, e.g., Tracey 1998, 262; Jakubowicz 2008, 277).

On the basis of our research on Nordic public broadcasting, we tend to take a different perspective on the situation for public service broadcasters. We have characterized Nordic public service broadcasters as resourceful, resilient, and adaptable to changing circumstances. In the Nordic region, public service broadcasters manage to use new technologies to revitalize their output and address new audiences. They clearly take their cues from commercial competitors, but adapt them to their own needs, and the broadcasters have also done a great deal to improve relations with policymakers, industry, and the public at large (Syvertsen 2008; Moe and Syvertsen 2009).

Our view of public service broadcasters as strong and resourceful is importantly not to be taken as a universal diagnosis. The Nordic public service broadcasters' characteristics—a central position in society, substantial public funding, a comprehensive and varied output, and authority as the voice of the nation—are dependent on political and public support within the wider context of the Nordic states and widespread support for welfare state solutions. As we have shown, the Nordic public broadcasters stand out in an international perspective, including to date in the digital age.

From Public Service Broadcasting to Public Service Media

The most important issue concerning the public service broadcasters in the second decade of the 21st century involves the transformation from public service broadcasting to public service media. While the incorporation of new media platforms is well documented, and while users are familiar with diverse output beyond radio and television, a full-blown recognition of a public service system for all electronic media is still missing. For the institutions, such a move means that they would have to rethink how they present their content—not least in terms of what commercial actors would call "the brand" or "the universe of services." The idea of serving one public with a carefully constructed program schedule—which was the original mode of the public service broadcasters in radio and television—simply does not suffice anymore, as the media landscape becomes more globalized and the audience more fragmented.

How the Nordic public service broadcasters will go about the transformation into (cross-)media providers is not only a question of organizational change and attractive content that the public responds to. It is also very clearly a political issue. While the national governments in the Nordic region have allowed the broadcasters to embrace the online world, in line with the regulatory tradition of flexibility and adaptability, the final move from "broadcasting" to "media" is still left wanting. For one thing, such a move could jeopardize the legitimacy of the up-until-now secure funding schemes that are dependent on political support. Furthermore, due to their comprehensive and ambitious online activities, the Nordic public service broadcasters have run into new competitors, a development that triggers reactions from competition authorities. Commercial online news actors across Europe are opposing further growth of public service media into what they see as their natural domain (e.g., Donders and Moe 2011). In a sense, the public service broadcasters are meeting marketization by expansion, as the ventures into online news have placed the institutions in a new and amorphous market situation. Hence, the future prospects of Nordic public service media depend on how the corporations manage to maneuver, both in the marketplace, but also to a large extent politically, sustaining their legitimacy as key institutions of the Media Welfare State.

Summary

We started this chapter by discussing the historical development of the Nordic public service broadcasters, arguing that more than any other media and communication structure public service broadcasting reflects the principles of the Media Welfare State: the organization of vital communication services as public goods, a cultural policy extended to media, editorial freedom, and cooperation between private and public stakeholders in the region. Along with the BBC, the Danish DR, the Finnish YLE, the Icelandic RÚV, the Norwegian NRK, and the Swedish SVT (and SR) all have a history as universalistic institutions that can be traced back to public radio services in the first part of the 20th century. In the 1950s and 1960s television services were included in the Nordic public service broadcasters' portfolios. In the 1970s new satellite technology emerged, and corporate interest groups lobbied for liberalization. This eventually led to the abolishing of the broadcasting monopolies, and the public service broadcasters began to compete with commercial television channels throughout the 1980s and 1990. While the digitalization of the networks in the 2000s provided an extended portfolio of niche channels, simultaneously, the Nordic public service broadcasters expanded their services to online platforms, both through the redistribution of programs and the production of a diverse range of original online content from digital games to weather forecasts. The concept of public service broadcasting has therefore become an umbrella that includes not only television and radio broadcasting, but also online services.

Summing up the chapter, we draw attention to three main points related to the Nordic public service broadcasters and the role they occupy in relation to the Media Welfare State.

The first point is that *universality* has remained a key ideal throughout the history of Nordic public service broadcasting. In return for a stable and secure source of income such as the license fee, the public service organizations are obliged not to serve only selected social groups, provide elite content, or supplement the output from commercial channels with the type of programs that tend not to survive in the marketplace. Rather, the opposite is the case, as the Nordic public service broadcasters are expected to serve the entire population and to be relevant for all age groups and every social segment. In the digital age, the tendencies toward fragmentation and the inclusion of niche channels in the portfolio both represent a key challenge for the public service broadcasters; they need to maintain their broad appeal and mixed programming, but at the same time, develop targeted products and services to reach new audiences.

Second, Nordic public service broadcasters have countered the challenges of marketization, fragmentation, and globalization with a strategy of *adaptability*, as they have been resilient without losing their characteristics. The transformation of public service broadcasting is a key case for how welfare state institutions, upheld by a certain combination of ideal principles and pragmatic solutions, change and adapt, but survive. Public service broadcasters changed significantly since their inception in the interwar period, but their services and output still remain distinct from those of purely commercial broadcasting. As the cases of online services and children's channels demonstrate, Nordic public service broadcasters are adaptive, and they have managed to, yet again, change in the face of new technologies.

A third point is related to new digital services and the future prospects for Nordic public service broadcasting. The chapter has demonstrated that the inclusion of online services in the remit poses new complications as it becomes more difficult to identify precisely what public service broadcasting is all about. Globalization and marketization make national public service organizations a difficult task to manage online. For example, services such as NRK's weather service, yr.no, are criticized for having a negative effect upon competition within the free trade regime of the European Union. Nordic public service broadcasting is restricted and enabled by national policies, but also by supranational policy and international restrictions on publicly supported media. The future of Nordic public service broadcasters depends on the organizations' continued adaptability, as well as on their ability to remain relevant in programming and services—to retain their position as central cultural institutions in a more fragmented and globalizing media environment.

// FIVE //

The Nordic Media Company

The media and communication system consists to a large extent of commercial businesses. In democratic societies, the press has always been a private enterprise. All of the Nordic countries' radio and television sectors have included commercial actors for more than three decades. Likewise, the telecom sector, incorporating Internet communication, is a commercial sector consisting of private and semiprivate companies.

The perspective of this book is that private and public institutions should not be seen as opposites, but rather as complementary. One of the hallmarks of the Media Welfare State is a successful private-public mix, but how can we more precisely understand the role of commercial firms within a Media Welfare State with a high level of regulation and state involvement?

The chapter discusses the role of private companies in the Nordic media and communications market. The main emphasis is on the fourth pillar of the Media Welfare State—the tendency toward consensual and cooperative solutions that involve all main stakeholders—although we also touch on the other three pillars. The discussion of the role of private media companies and the forms of private-public cooperation is based on three cases, which are chosen to represent different types of corporations:

Schibsted is a Norwegian publishing house that has expanded to other sectors and is internationally based on strength in a national newspaper market. Schibsted is currently one of the global leaders in the online classified advertisements market.

The *Modern Times Group* grew out of an industrial company that expanded into media and communications, with an explicit agenda to break up monopolies and challenge public regulation. The Modern Times Group and its subsidiaries constitute a strong international player in radio, television, and free newspapers.

Nokia is the Finnish hardware manufacturer that grew to prominence as the world's largest producer of mobile phones, but that in later years has faced major setbacks due to competition from Apple and other smartphone producers.

All three companies took advantage of the new business opportunities arising in media and communication from the 1970s and 1980s and expanded significantly in the 1990s and 2000s. They combine a prominent role in national and Nordic markets with an extensive overseas expansion. Indeed, a significant number of media companies emerging from the Nordic region have become well-known brand names and have performed commercially well around the world. This may seem paradoxical given that we are speaking of a region of five small states, usually known for their extensive state control.

This chapter charts the strategic expansion of the three companies both nationally and internationally and discusses their relationship with the state and the policy regimes of the Media Welfare State. Although the companies in many respects have followed similar strategies, their modus operandi can also be used to exemplify their differences. In this chapter, we use Schibsted to exemplify what we have termed an *adaptive* strategy, the Kinnevik/Modern Times Group to exemplify a *confrontational* strategy, and Nokia to exemplify a *collaborative* strategy. Mapping various strategies is important not only in order to understand the companies, but also to understand the evolvement of market structures and the forms of private-public collaboration in the region.

The chapter has six parts. Following this introduction, part 2 discusses the characteristics of media firms in a changing marketplace and some general traits related to Nordic media and communications companies. The next three parts focus on the cases of Schibsted, the Modern Times Group, and Nokia, respectively, while the last part summarizes the main findings.

Opportunities and Challenges for Private Companies

Like other markets, the Nordic media market is also going through major transformation—technological, economic, structural, and political. The transformation of production, distribution, and consumption over the last few decades has opened new lines of business, while also posing difficult challenges for media companies.

One major factor is convergence and digitalization, which breaks down boundaries between sectors, products, and services. Companies worldwide have responded by expanding their operations across sectors, and the last decades have seen an unprecedented global wave of mergers and acquisitions (Doyle 2013; Ozanich and Wirth 2004). With convergence, there has been a strong push toward maximizing the number of "windows," i.e. to leverage content over an increased number of distribution channels (Ozanich and Wirth 2004, 77). The new conglomerates strive to exploit economies of scale and scope in a market that requires large capital investments. To be a player in the new media markets, the understanding has been that one must be enlarged, diversified, and vertically integrated (Doyle 2013, 15–22).

As elsewhere, expansion comes in waves in the Nordic countries. The discussion of specific strategies later in the chapter charts the development through three loosely defined phases. The first phase comprises the preliminary developments in the 1970s and early 1980s, when companies both in and out of the sector made their first investments in media and communications outside their core areas. The next phase comprises the great expansion in the 1990s and early 2000s, when a number of players established themselves in new markets opened up by reregulation and the liberalization of telecommunications and broadcasting, and later online markets (Sundin 2013, 9). In the third and last phase, the general trend is toward consolidation and expansion in some core areas, with Sundin (2013) dating this last change for most Nordic media and communications companies to approximately 2005.

Hand in hand with the vertical and horizontal expansion is the tendency toward international expansion, and in the last two decades of the 20th century, the rapid expansion of media companies into global markets dramatically reshaped the industry. Particularly dramatic was the globalization of the electronic media: telephone, television, radio, and cable (Hollifield 2004, 85). Until the 1980s these media sectors were largely domestic industries dominated by publicly regulated companies (Ulset and Gooderham 2000; Thue 2006, 10; From 2009, 24). From the late 1970s, advances in communication technology allowed parent companies to quickly exchange information with foreign-based subsidiaries, thereby making it easier to coordinate far-flung operations and move products along great distances (Hollifield 2004, 88–89). In addition, a number of Asian and Latin American countries have evolved into strong consumer economies with a growing demand for media and communication products, creating opportunities for foreign direct investments, international joint ventures, and content export. Since 1989, the collapse of the Eastern bloc has opened new investment opportunities in Central and Eastern Europe (Hollifield 2004, 90). Nordic companies have exploited these opportunities and expanded in all of these markets.

The premise in this chapter is that these changes cannot only be studied on a macro level. To understand the Nordic political economy in media and communications, as well as the evolvement of the Media Welfare State, it is also important to investigate the role of companies. As Hall and Soskice (2011, 6–7) argue, firms are a prominent unit to analyze in order to understand the political economy in a region, not least because the capabilities of companies are ultimately relational; a company's degree of success will substantially depend on its ability to coordinate effectively with a range of other actors. In their typology of political economies, Hall and Soskice (2001, 8, 19) place the Nordic countries in a category labelled as coordinated market economies along with Germany, Austria, Switzerland, the Netherlands, Belgium, and Japan. Their characteristic feature is the high degree of coordination and interdependence between individual firms, as well as a more extensive coordination with the state than in liberal market economies. Key actors are encouraged "to engage in collective discussion and reach agreements with each other" (Hall and Soskice 2001, 11).

However, also within the overall structure of collaboration, firms may be different. While the quest for profit is integrated as the very rationale of large firms, firms may also pursue noneconomic goals that may differ from company to company. For example, media and communication companies may wish to have political influence or to sustain status as a prestigious national cornerstone institution. Firms also differ more concretely in the ways they are operated. Some firms are dominated by their owners and managed with a more personal flair, while others are run by top management, which may be more or less collaborative and collective (Doyle 2013, 5–8). Moreover, these characteristics impinge on the relationships with other actors and the state.

Large private companies represent dilemmas for the state and policymakers, both in the Nordic countries and elsewhere. In many ways the relationship between the state and large communications enterprises is characterized by ambiguity and ambivalence.

On the one hand, governments are dependent on a strong business sector, as large companies generate employment and tax income. In the Nordic countries, there has also been a view that strong media and communication companies are important as a bulwark against foreign ownership, which is in accordance with the cultural policy and its emphasis on the media as vehicles of nation-building and identity. In general, the strength of the domestic and Nordic companies has served as an important protection against foreign dominance. Although several of the world's media companies are represented in the Nordic market through subsidiaries, and not least through media products, Nordic players dominate. Among the 20 largest media companies by revenue in the Nordic market in 2012, there were only 2 that were non-Nordic, the British Mecom and the German ProSiebenSat (Sundin 2013, 15).

A second positive factor for governments is that large communication companies act as drivers of innovation and growth and have specifically been vehicles to turn the Nordic countries into advanced information societies. Although large companies can be barriers to innovation, economic theory suggests that strong market conditions and even a monopoly may give firms the type of protection they need to dare to make risky investments. Additionally, regulations such as restrictions on ownership may lead to "choking off" investments in new infrastructure and limit product innovation (Doyle 2013, 179).

On the other hand, large media and communication companies represent problems for government. Within the context of the policy regime we have called the Media Welfare State, the overall view is that large companies, namely the concentration of ownership, pose threats to pluralism and diversity (Syvertsen 2004). Generally speaking, intervention by governments is called for to restrict the exercise of monopoly power, which is considered particularly important when the plurality of views and opinions is put into question (Doyle 2013, 167–69). For policymakers and governments, it is difficult to determine if and how to intervene in the media market. Yet, as a rule, if not restricted, large companies will expand their operations and try to achieve economies of both scale and scope (Doyle 2013, 188–90).

In this chapter, we explore the political duality between restricting and enabling large private companies to dominate and expand. We discuss the expansionist strategies of our three Nordic cases and their collaboration (and noncollaboration) with the state and other operators and how the companies combine their Nordic role with international expansion.

Schibsted: Innovation through Adaption

Schibsted is the largest media company in Norway, the fourth largest in the Nordic region, and has international operations in approximately 30 countries. The company has a combined share of 32 percent of the newspaper circulation in Norway and 15 percent in Sweden and owns the largest paper in both countries (Nordicom 2012b). Schibsted's holdings include free, paid, and online newspapers, in addition to online classified services in Europe, Latin America, Asia, and Africa. Schibsted is the largest European player in the classified market (Sundin 2013, 71), competing globally with the US companies eBay and Craigslist. In 2009, Schibsted consolidated their Norwegian media interests, including four of the largest regional newspapers, into a joint company and created a similar construction for their publishing and Internet interests in Sweden (Sundin 2013, 71; see table 5.1).

A Cornerstone Institution

Schibsted plays a significant role in Norwegian and Nordic public life. Its strong editorial position, including its adherence to the principle of editorial freedom, as well as its innovative and adaptive attitude toward change, makes it an important player within the context of the Media Welfare State. Like the public service broadcaster NRK, Schibsted can be likened in Norway to a cornerstone institution, running the two largest newspapers, operating as a book publisher responsible for the Norwegian version of *Who's Who*, and also being a significant force in the start-up of commercial television. Schibsted's Norwegian activities reach three out of four Norwegians every day (MedieNorge 2013a), and half the population of Sweden (Schibsted 2013a). At the same time, Schibsted is an expansive capitalist company that has been seen by policymakers and others as a threat to diversity and pluralism, and it has had to adapt its strategies so as to secure political legitimacy.

Schibsted's main channel of influence on the Norwegian public sphere is through its newspapers, of which the most important, *Aftenposten*, can trace its roots back to 1860 (Norland 2001, 2011). Throughout the years of the party press, *Aftenposten* was a conservative paper, its nickname "Auntie" signifying its careful and bourgeois editorial position. In line with the process of depoliticization, the conservative stamp on the paper gradually disappeared (e.g. Norland 2011, 209ff.), and in recent years its editors have held widely divergent political convictions. Schibsted's adaptability in this respect is illuminated by the fact that it has a majority share in the Swedish *Aftonbladet*, which

TABLE 5.1. Schibsted

Established	1836 in Norway by Christian Michael Schibsted
Original business	Family-owned publishing company
Key businesses (2012)	Subscription newspapers, single copy newspapers, free newspapers, online news, online classified ads, book publishing
Employees (2012)	Approximately 7,800 in 29 countries
Total net sales (2012)	€1.960 mill.
Geographical key areas (2012)	Norway, Sweden, France, Spain, Italy, Austria, Ireland. Also has investments in other European countries, as well as the Philippines, Indonesia, Malaysia, Brazil, Chile, and Morocco.
Reach, examples (2012)	• Approximately 75 percent of the Norwegian population over the age of 12 use one or more of Schibsted's media channels daily. • Schibsted's international (outside Norway) online classified websites had over 14 billion page views in the span of only one month. • *20 Minutes*, the free newspaper, is distributed in 40 cities in France. Altogether, 12.7 million people read the print and digital versions of *20 Minutes* each month.

Source: Schibsted 2012; MedieNorge 2013a; Nordicom 2012b; TNS Gallup 2012.

is a Social-Democratic paper of which the other proprietor is the Swedish Trade Union Confederation (Barland 2012, 6ff.).

The strong editorial position and competence of Schibsted have been important for its later expansionist strategy, particularly in relation to its buying newspapers and television companies. However, just as important for its later expansion were the company's strong commercial foundations, particularly its unbeatable position in the advertising market. An important historical explanation for its later strength is that *Aftenposten* continued to be published during World War II, when Norway was occupied by Nazi Germany (Norland 2011, 57ff.). After World War II, Schibsted had to pay compensation to the state, but their position was never again eroded (e.g., Hjeltnes 2010, 20ff.). Hence, Schibsted was not affected by the "newspaper deaths" in the 1950s and 1960s; instead, its strong position can explain why other papers died.

Strategy and Expansion

Schibsted's strong economic position has been important for what can be seen as its three main waves of expansion. The first wave began in 1966 when Schibsted acquired its second Norwegian newspaper, *Verdens Gang*—which for several decades was the Nordic region's best-selling newspaper (Norland 2011, 200ff.). During the 1970s and 1980s, Schibsted gradually strengthened its position in the national and regional newspaper markets (e.g., Hjeltnes 2010, 421ff.).

The listing of the company on the Norwegian stock exchange in 1992 indicated the beginning of the second wave and a new and rapid wave of expansion. Schibsted rapidly moved into television and film and began acquiring shares in other Nordic media companies (Norland 2001; Dahl 2003). In 1991, it was one of the founders of Norwegian TV2 (Norland 2011, 303–4), with the company subsequently buying into Swedish TV4 and Finnish Alma Media (Sundin 2013, 71). In 1996, Schibsted began to buy into the Swedish newspaper market, and two years later it acquired a majority position in Estonia's biggest newspaper. In 1999, it also launched free newspapers in Switzerland and Germany (Norland 2011, 305; see also chap. 3).

Newspapers, film, and television have all been important for strengthening Schibsted's capital base. Yet, it is Schibsted's online services, and particularly the classified market, that have been its most expansive area in recent years. As early as 1996, Schibsted established an Internet portal for Scandinavian users, which within two years became the most visited website in Sweden and Norway. This was also a strategic maneuver to prevent foreign, and in particular US, companies from settling in Scandinavia (Cedergren 2007). In 1999, the company invested in e-commerce and e-auction services, founding

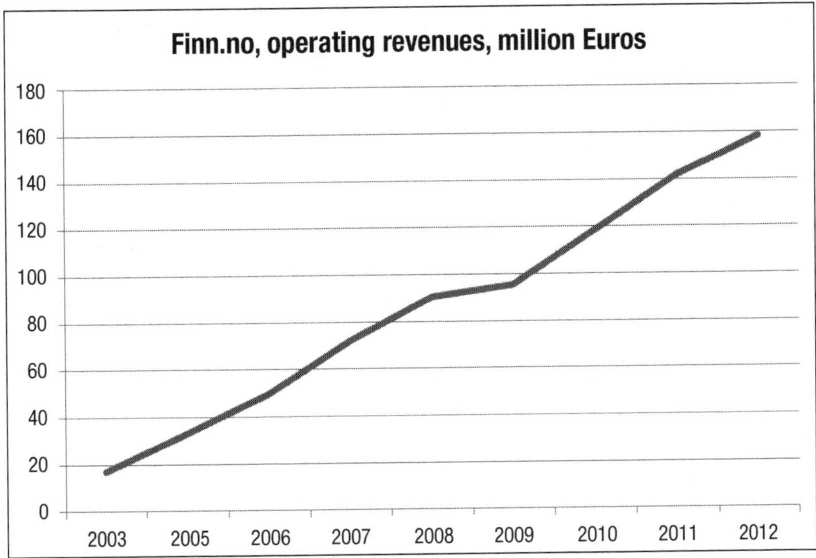

Fig. 5.1. Finn.no online classifieds: Operating revenues in million Euros. (Data from Schibsted 2003, 2005, 2007, 2008, 2010, 2012.)

the classified advertising site finn.no, which became a huge success. Figure 5.1 illustrates the growth in the operational revenues of finn.no.

In 2003, a parallel Swedish service was acquired. The company took the success of their Nordic services as an indication of a global growth potential, rapidly launching similar services in more than 20 countries (Barland 2012, 161). The strategy was to identify "green markets," where the lack of competition would make it possible to rapidly acquire and sustain market dominance.

The late 1990s represented top years for Schibsted, in which the company increased its profitability in almost all operating areas, not least in its multimedia division. However, around 2005 the strategy changed. After meeting difficulties in the television market and problems in obtaining operational control in its television companies, Schibsted decided to sell its film and television interests (Sundin 2013, 71).

The transition to the third phase is marked by Schibsted's decision to focus more on core areas, the traditional area of publishing and the new core area of online classified advertising. The period of broad expansion, in which all large companies seemed to compete in all major markets, was nearing the end, and many companies consolidated their interests in the markets where they were most successful. As areas of operation narrowed, ambitions rose. Self-confidently, the company changed its vision from that of being "Scandinavia's leading media company" (Schibsted 1995, 6) to "being the most attractive media company in Europe" (Schibsted 2005, 2).

The Adaptive Company

In many ways, Schibsted has been a privileged media institution. The company's reputation as a responsible and adaptive operator and the fact that its strength has prevented international operators from gaining a foothold are explanations as to why it has received political and economic support in many instances.

Although Schibsted does not enjoy direct press support, the full tax exemption for printed papers is an important form of subsidy in Norway. Print journalism is exempted because of the press's important role in the public sphere, but the tax exemption benefits not only pluralism and quality journalism, but also the shareholders (e.g., Hjeltnes 2010, 456). The strong position of Schibsted as a responsible corporation also helps to explain why Schibsted's consortium of interests received a license in 1991 for TV2, the first nationwide Norwegian television channel. TV2 was privileged in the sense that it was the only television channel to distribute advertising on a national scale. With a solid economy as a basis (Dahl 2003), Schibsted's legitimacy as a responsible publisher and national cornerstone institution was seen as reassuring, and so also was their application with plans for a serious editorial profile for the new channel (Syvertsen 1997, 34–35).

But Schibsted is not only supported, its expansionist strategies in newspapers and television have been seen to threaten pluralism. After a "responsible" beginning, the new television channel TV2, which was owned in part by Schibsted, adopted a more outright commercial strategy, soon turning the channel into a "license to print money" (Dahl 2003, 184). The relationship between the company and political authorities deteriorated, and toward the end of the first franchise period, the owners were explicitly warned that the license might not be renewed (Syvertsen 2006, 52). Parallel to this development, there was great concern about Schibsted buying into local and regional newspapers, and in 1997 an ownership ceiling was introduced that prevented any company from growing beyond one-third of any specific market, with an aim of ensuring freedom of expression and media pluralism (Syvertsen 2004, 159). That the law was designed to limit Schibsted's domestic expansion was so obvious that commentators named it Lex Schibsted; the company already had a 32 percent share of the national newspaper circulation and a significant share in TV2, and it was well known that it planned to continue to expand (Syvertsen 2004, 173).

Schibsted has been well aware of, and concerned about, the threats to its legitimacy. In television, the company adapted to meet the political criticism and made a complete turnaround before the franchise expired; a new and more acceptable CEO was brought in, and cultural and public service programming was boosted (Syvertsen 2006 52ff.). Having secured renewal of the television franchise, and thus protecting its investment, Schibsted subsequently sold out of TV2 in 2006 with a large profit, simultaneously also selling its television holdings in other Nordic countries (Schibsted 2013b).

In the newspaper market, political restrictions have also posed problems for Schibsted. It was only in 2009, after a prolonged period of negotiation with state agencies, that the company was permitted to take control over a range of regional newspapers and construct a consolidated company. The move required Schibsted to adapt on several counts, including the selling of shares in other media companies. Nevertheless, the merger continued to attract criticism, and in accordance with historical precedents, Schibsted adopted a proactive defense strategy, arguing the benefits of the move in letters to the editor and posts on the op-ed space in papers other than its own.

Schibsted's answer to the criticism is that their expansion and mergers benefit the public good, safeguarding employment in the media sector and leading to "better newspapers," according to Rolv Erik Ryssdal, the CEO of Schibsted (Ryssdal 2011a, authors' translation). Public hearings are an important collaborative institution in the Nordic countries, and Schibsted takes its role seriously in such proceedings, publicly defending the benefits of its maneuvers in different media markets. In a public submission about ownership regulations, Ryssdal argues that Norwegian media proprietors do not pose, and have not posed, a threat to freedom of speech or pluralism, since "The deep respect for editorial independence is a key reason for the media houses' success and high circulation" (Ryssdal 2011b, authors' translation). Instead, according to Ryssdal, the real problem is that political restrictions lead to less robust media companies and that in the current structural upheavals, "more newspapers will fail" (Ryssdal 2011b, authors' translation).

While Schibsted is proud to act as a bulwark to foreign ownership in the Nordic countries, it sees its own expansion in another light, arguing that it aids editorial freedom through its newspaper holdings in countries with a weaker tradition of free speech, such as in the former Eastern Europe (e.g., Schibsted 2013c). It is also a fact that Schibsted's own ownership structure has become more international in recent years. Still, in 2013 Schibsted sold Eesti Meedia, its Baltic media operation, which consisted of newspapers, magazines, and television and radio stations, as well as online classified ads (Sundin 2013).

Accordingly, Schibsted is an innovative company with economic growth as a key goal, but also with the noneconomic goal of being a national cornerstone institution. Schibsted has chosen an adaptive strategy in its relations with the state and has benefitted in turn from a high legitimacy in the public domain, justified by the firm's profile as a protector of free speech and a bulwark against foreign ownership.

Modern Times Group: Innovation through Confrontation

The Modern Times Group (MTG) was formed in 1994 out of the media holdings of the Swedish investment company Kinnevik. The company and its many subsidiaries and associates (which are all discussed here under the name of Modern Times Group) span activities on four continents. The subsidiary, Viasat Broadcasting, transmits approximately 60 television channels to markets in the Nordic countries, the Baltic countries, Eastern Europe, and Russia, as well as some other areas. Commercial radio networks are operated in Sweden, Norway, and the Baltic countries. The portfolio further includes Strix, a leading Nordic television production company; the subsidiary Metro International, which runs free newspapers; and the e-commerce subsidiary CDON. The company is also involved in the Pan-European telecom operator Tele2 and the digital service provider company Millicom (Sundin 2013, 77; see table 5.2).

TABLE 5.2. Modern Times Group

Established	1936 in Sweden by Hugo Stenbeck as *Kinnevik*
Original business	Investment company (forest and steel industry)
Employees (2012)	Approximately 3,000 in 18 countries
Key businesses (2012)	Free TV, pay TV, radio, television production studios
Total net sales (2012)	€1.560 million
Geographical key areas (2012)	The Nordic region, the Baltics, Russia, Ukraine, the Czech Republic, Bulgaria, Hungary, and Ghana. Additionally, the company has redistribution of television channels in 31 countries across Central and Eastern Europe, Africa, and North America.
Reach, examples (2012)	• Modern Times Group's Swedish free-to-air television channels have a combined share of viewing of 34.8 percent. In the Baltic countries, the Modern Times Group has between 40 and 60 percent of combined share of viewing (target audience 15–49). • The Modern Times Group has over 1 million premium subscribers in the Nordic countries. Through third-party television redistribution, the Modern Times Group channels reach 84 million subscriptions. • The Modern Times Group is the largest for-profit radio operator in both the Nordic region and the Baltic countries and reaches over 3 million radio listeners daily.

Source: MTG 2012.

A Nordic Media Mogul

The forestry and steel company Kinnevik can stand as an example of a relative newcomer in the media markets, an industrial group with no roots in traditional publishing that moved into media and communications in pursuit of profit. The company's base for the large-scale investments in media and communications was the profitable industrial enterprises outside the media sector (Sundin 2013, 77). The cash-rich investment company further stands as the best example of a large Nordic media enterprise that stood, and continues to stand, outside the welfare state consensus and culture, instead coming from the outside with an explicit goal of creating an outright commercial system. Many of the maneuvers have been successful, and the company can be seen as one of those who most distinctly contributed to reshaping and liberalizing the Nordic systems of communication.

The expansion into media and communications is due in large part to the strategic drive of the CEO, Jan Stenbeck (1942–2002), who inherited the company in 1976 and shortly thereafter made the first moves into telecom and media. Jan Stenbeck saw great potential for profit in media and communication, though at the time these sectors were strictly regulated, with monopolies in both telecommunication and broadcasting. Jan Stenbeck is perhaps the closest we get to identifying a Nordic media mogul insofar as resembling international counterparts such as Rupert Murdoch, the controlling owner of News Corp., and Silvio Berlusconi, the former prime minister of Italy and a controversial media proprietor. The comparisons are based on Jan Stenbeck's controversial personality and personal leadership style, the way he has confronted regulation, and his overall controversial methods. Stenbeck's style was inspired by his long stays in United States, where he drew inspiration from a more competitive and private-initiative-focused business culture than in the Nordic region (Andersson 2000).

Strategy and Expansion

The Modern Times Group (and its predecessors and subsidiaries) has had a formative influence on most Nordic media and communication markets, including telecom, broadcasting, publishing, and content production. There have been several waves of investments, and again we can loosely divide them into three phases.

The first phase comprises the very beginnings in the 1970s and 1980s, when the media and communications markets were still characterized by public monopolies, and the moves in this phase can be seen as a precondition for later investments. Stenbeck inherited the company in 1976 and shortly after that began to buy up small companies operating communication networks for car phones. These investments served as a basis for the establishment in 1981 of Comvik, the first European cellular telephone company to challenge the state telephone monopoly (Garrard 1998). This pioneering initiative would later give the company advantages in both the Nordic and international mobile/telecom markets, and telecom licenses were acquired in emerging markets such as Mauritius, Sri Lanka, Pakistan, and Hong Kong (Andersson 2000, 236). In particular, the Hong Kong license turned out to be lucrative, and it was sold in 1991 for approximately 10–15 times the initial investment (Andersson 2000, 237). In 1992, Comvik was renamed Comviq to coincide with the shift to the GSM network, and five years later the company merged with Tele2.

In the first phase, the company also made crucial investments in television through its investments in the Astra satellite in the early 1980s (Sundin 2013, 77). On New Year's Eve, Stenbeck simultaneously launched the pan-Scandinavian satellite channel TV3 in Norway, Sweden, and Denmark, challenging the national broadcasting monopolies in all three countries (Syvertsen 1992, 204). The production company Strix was simultaneously launched to produce more outright commercial programming. From the beginning Strix confronted good taste with risqué and controversial formats.

The second phase commenced in the 1990s, when the company significantly broadened its investments. From the beginning, the focus was on building vertically integrated chains involving all levels from content production to distribution by satellite or cable. Within television, there was a broad expansion with start-ups and the acquisition of channels in the Nordic countries, the Baltic countries, Eastern Europe, and Russia (Sundin 2013, 77). The first pay television channel was launched in 1989, marking the company's efforts to obtain independence from advertising (Sundin 2013, 77). The Modern Times Group won the franchise to run the first nationwide commercial radio in Norway in 1993, which was an investment that was to become very profitable (Enli and Sundet 2007). When private local radio was introduced in Sweden during the same year, Kinnevik acquired a number of licenses that were brought together in a centralized network (Sundin 2013, 77). Two years later, in 1995, the free print newspaper *Metro* was introduced. At its height in 2009, local versions of *Metro* reached 19 million readers through 56 daily editions in 18 countries worldwide (Parmann 2010; see chap. 3). In 1997, the Modern Times Group was listed on the Stockholm stock exchange and NASDAQ in New York (MTG 2012).

The transition to the third phase was marked by the death of CEO Jan Stenbeck in 2002. The company was taken over by his daughter and continued with broadly the same strategy, but the Modern Times Group (with associates and subsidiaries) was also narrowed and its operations consolidated. Several peripheral businesses were liquidated, and there was a concentration around core business areas. The Nordic presence continued to grow, but the bulk of the growth took place in Eastern Europe. A number of *Metro* newspapers were sold (Sundin 2013, 78). In 2013, Metro has only been published in seven countries and in Sweden; the company has given up their nationwide ambitions, focusing instead on selected metropolitan markets (77). Like other companies, the Modern Times Group has focused on digital markets and new revenue sources, with an increase in online revenues of 9 percent per year.

The Confrontational Company

We have identified a tradition for cooperation between private and public shareholders as a key characteristic of the Media Welfare State, though Stenbeck's companies are an exception to the rule. Throughout their history, the companies have openly confronted consensual principles, political regulation, monopolies, and the cultural elite, in addition to standing for a commercial and populist business logic that is unparalleled in Nordic media history. The Modern Times Group and its predecessors and associates constitute an interesting case, both because they provide a contrast to other operators and because they have been an important force in the reshaping of Nordic media.

Three characteristics can describe the confrontational style. First, the company has entered the market from outside and established independent vertical supply chains that allow it to produce, package, and distribute its own content, and on the basis of these structures it challenged existing monopolies and policies. The company used surprising and audacious moves, frequently in alliance with populist media and right-wing parties that have needed a lever to bring about political change. The company does not bend to political pressure, but moves boldly ahead without budging. Moreover, these tactics can also be seen in telecom, television, and radio.

In telecom, the 1981 launch of the mobile telephone company Comvik came as a surprise to other operators, the launch being only a week prior to the official opening of the state telecom's Nordic mobile telephone network (NMT) standard. The move was highly controversial because Comvik benefitted from a standard initiated by the state and the dominant private telecom players (e.g., Ericsson) and because the move openly confronted the state telecom monopoly—a cornerstone of the universal Nordic communication structures. There was also considerable political and public pressure to stop Comvik, but since Stenbeck already maintained an alternative telecom network, the authorities had few alternatives. Although permission to operate was granted, the company remained controversial (Karlsson 1998, 238ff.; Garrard 1998).

In television, Stenbeck also applied a surprise tactic to crush public monopolies. In 1987, distribution of domestic advertising to viewers in Norway, Sweden, and Denmark was still prohibited, and policymakers were debating whether to liberalize and under what conditions. This ban also applied to Stenbeck's plan to establish a pan-Scandinavian television channel to begin on New Year's Eve. Aided by large advertisements in Scandinavian newspapers, claiming that the start-up of TV3 was the most exciting event since the beginning of television, Stenbeck managed to raise a wave of populist support, and the ban was eventually lifted. On New Year's Eve in 1987, Stenbeck's TV3 pioneered the broadcast of Scandinavian commercial television run from the London headquarters to viewers in Norway, Sweden, and Denmark (Syvertsen 1992, 204). Nonetheless, TV3 continued to be a thorn in the eye of Nordic television authorities since it refused to comply with national advertising regulations; instead, it operated according to the much more liberal regulations in Great Britain.

Stenbeck's radio tactics were also highly confrontational. We have seen that the Modern Times Group was involved in the franchise for the first Norwegian commercial radio channel with public service obligations, P4, in 1993. P4 was organized as a parallel structure to the television channel TV2, and like TV2, P4 was soon criticized for being too commercial and neglecting its cultural and public service obligations (Enli and Sundet 2007). However, in contrast to Schibsted and TV2, the Modern Times Group and P4 did not adapt to political pressure and openly demonstrated that they would not oblige. Norwegian media authorities clearly wanted to set an example, and in 2003 the franchise was awarded to another operator (Enli and Sundet 2007, 712ff.). Following loud protests and a heated public debate, P4 was granted permission to broadcast on a more limited frequency, and in a bold and surprising move, it stopped broadcasting on the original frequency, thereby forcing listeners to move along before the new operator was ready to take over. As a result, P4 managed to move most of its listener base to its new station, leaving the market entrant with the difficult task of building a listener base from scratch (Enli and Sundet 2007). In the years to follow, P4 remained the more successful of the two stations.

The second, and related, confrontational trait can be found in the company's thoroughly commercial business culture and the stubborn focus on entertainment. The company's program profile can almost be seen as anti-diversity, openly confronting the Nordic cultural policy consensus and the understanding that media should not just entertain but benefit the public as citizens. Although some of the company's media outlets started out with a more diverse profile, diversity was soon reduced (Sundin 2013, 78; Ihlebæk et al. 2011). The radio channels run by the company are dominated by strictly formatted music radio (Sundin 2013, 78). The free daily newspaper, *Metro*, can be seen as the antidote to the established Nordic press, both in terms of production, business model, and distribution model and in terms of journalistic content (Andersson 2000; Gustafsson and Rydén 2010, 323; see chap. 3). The commercial entertainment culture is seen not least in the television programming repertoire of Strix, the production company started in 1988 that specialized in controversial reality-TV formats, including *The Bar* (Baren) and *The Farm* (Farmen), both of which were exported internationally, as well as the global success of *Survivor* (Expedition Robinson).

From early on, TV3 challenged established norms with these shows, in addition to talk shows in which guests were seen swearing, drinking, and even fighting. These formats were widely criticized in the Swedish and Scandinavian press and were understood as a head-on attack on cultural policy principles. Strix still recurrently exploits the criticism to brand themselves as an innovative, fearless, and cutting-edge production company, both when publicly defending their formats and when promoting the company:

> It's been said that Strix is the industry's maverick. It's been said that Strix is the true underdog. We can live with that. We know who we are. Strix is a unique company with a strong journalistic backbone, combined with a remarkably strong desire to engage and entertain. (Strix 2013)

The third confrontational trait is linked with the company's personal and mogul-like leadership, which differed tremendously from the usual Nordic style, as Jan Stenbeck dominated the company to a level that is unusual in companies this size (Sundin 2013, 78). In the same way as Rupert Murdoch's Sky Channel broke new ground and challenged the postwar regime (Andersson 2000, 254), Stenbeck challenged the postwar Media Welfare State, diagnosing the Nordic markets as "the most undertelevised countries in the world" (Andersson 2000, 245). Many of the more responsible companies refused to support Stenbeck, although they benefitted from the liberalization of the media and communications markets. In the search for partners in early commercial television, major companies in the region such as Aller, Bonnier, and Schibsted were approached, but they were all reluctant to invest in an undeveloped and politically restricted market. Stenbeck saw himself as a loner, fighting on behalf of a greater good: "No one wanted to be the first in the boat. I was alone in the Scandinavian boat" (Andersson 2000, 245).

The story of the Modern Times Group illustrates how the construction of the Media Welfare State constrains private companies and how policy measures have been confronted and changed over the last decades. It also illuminates how formerly regulated markets may represent golden opportunities for risky and well-timed investments.

Nokia: Innovation through Collaboration

The Finnish company Nokia is perhaps the most well-known Nordic brand. From 1998 to 2012, Nokia was the world's largest manufacturer of mobile phones and employed approximately 100,000 people worldwide. Nokia's core business has been in three areas: smart devices and mobile phones, location-based products, and services such as digital map data and network technology and services (see table 5.3). Since 2007 and the launch of Apple's first Iphone, Nokia's operating profits dropped dramatically, and in 2013, Nokia's Devices & Services business—including its mobile phone operations—was sold to the information technology giant Microsoft (Microsoft 2013; Nokia 2013b).

The Hardware Manufacturer

Nokia's roots go back to 1865 and a riverside paper mill in southwestern Finland. The innovative company invested in the early 1900s in cable and electric

TABLE 5.3. Nokia Group

Established	1865 in Finland by Fredrik Idestam
Original business	Paper products manufacturer
Employees (2012)	Approximately 100,000 worldwide
Key businesses (2012)	Mobile phones, smart phones and related devices, apps and data services, mobile broadband network services
Total net sales (2012)	€30.176 million
Geographical key areas (2012)	In order of descending size: Europe, Asia-Pacific, Latin America, Middle East and Africa, Greater China, and North America
Reach, examples	• For 14 years after 1998, Nokia was the world's biggest manufacturer of mobile phones, shipping 83 million in 2012 alone. • In 2005, Nokia sells its billionth phone in Nigeria, and global mobile phone subscriptions pass 2 billion. Two years later, Nokia is recognized as the 5th most valued brand in the world. • Over 1.3 billion customers used Nokia devices in 2012.

Sources: Nokia Group 2012; BBC 2012; Nokia 2013a.

power, branching into electronics in the 1960s. The year 1963 saw the first move to telecom and mobile telephony as the company began to develop radio phones for the army and emergency services, and in the 1970s Nokia started to produce its own computers and developed digital telephone exchanges (Goggin 2006, 42; Nokia 2013a).

Nokia's growth and expansion from these modest beginnings must be understood in light of the Finnish state's involvements and investment in telecommunications. Although Nokia cannot be said to be a cornerstone of the Media Welfare State, it can in many ways be seen as a product of welfare state policies and a collaborative and consensual leadership style. The Finnish labor market provided Nokia with a large pool of well-educated engineers and designers, the company drew seed money out of public funding agencies, and long-term technology programs and the overall regulatory environment encouraged innovation in telecommunications (Castells and Himanen 2002, 54–55; Moen and Lilja 2005, 360–61).

In contrast to Stenbeck's company, which openly confronted national telecoms, Nokia has formed partnerships throughout its history and benefitted from close cooperation with public telecommunication companies, institutions, and agencies. For example, Nokia formed a joint telephone exchange venture in 1978 with another major Finnish telecommunications manufacturer, the state-owned phone company Televa Oy—which Nokia took over nine years later (Goggin 2006, 42).

Strategy and Expansion

Nokia has been a pioneer in the Nordic region and has had a tremendous impact on the way today's global community understands the mobile phone. For Nokia, we also chart three waves of expansion.

The first wave is the early investments, which are preconditions for later expansion. As we have previously shown, the dramatic changes in telecommunications and broadcasting began around 1980. Nokia was an early mover, creating the radio telephone company Mobira Oy in 1979 as a joint venture with the leading Finnish television set maker Salora and introducing the first car phone and digital telephone three years later. In 1987, Nokia introduced the first handheld mobile phone for the Nordic Mobile Telephone System network, which was the first international automatic network for mobile telephones (Moen and Lilja 2005, 362). Along with the new network, the first handheld phone indicated a significant wave of innovation.

The second wave of expansion occurred in 1992 when Nokia made a strategic decision to focus exclusively on telecommunications and mobile telephony, selling off its rubber, cable, and consumer electronics divisions.

Nokia's transformation was a response to the company's own overinvestments in consumer electronics, the recession in Europe, and increasing competition from the Asian producers of consumer electronics (Moen and Lilja 2005, 360). The collapse of the Eastern bloc also led to a serious downturn in the Finnish economy, since the Soviet Union had been a major market for Finnish companies. In 1992, Nokia changed its management and moved from being an industrial company to an informational company, announcing that it was to become "telecom-oriented, global, focused and value-added" (Castells and Himanen 2002, 30–31). Both globally and in Europe, telecom networks were liberalized in the 1990s, partly as a result of pressure from large corporations wanting to exploit a converging market for information and communication technologies (Thue 2006, 22; Thussu 2006, 67; Iosifidis 2011, 127).

From this moment, a key explanation for Nokia's success in the global market was their decision to transform the mobile telephone into a consumer product. The company's success was based on personalizing mobile phones and targeting different consumer markets (Moen and Lilja 2005, 361; see Pulkkinen 1997; Steinbock 2005, 56–58). At an early stage, Nokia understood the importance of fashion and entertainment in the market for mobile phones. For example, while the competing Swedish mobile phone company Ericsson produced neutral, practical handsets, Nokia opted for flashy colors and fun ringtones, designed for customers with a taste for fashion, and for entertainment and leisure use rather than primarily for business (Peters 1992; Andersson 2000, 241). By 1998, Nokia was launching new mobile telephone models every 35 days (Steinbock 2005, 57), hence becoming the world leader in mobile phones. Between 1996 and 2001, the company's turnover increased from €6.5 billion to €31 billion—an increase of nearly 500 percent (Nokia 2013a).

With the new millennium, mobile telephones began to emerge with web-based functions, including e-mail and cameras. The launch of the first 3G phone (third generation) in 2002 turned the mobile phone into a multipurpose terminal to be used for browsing the web, downloading music, watching audiovisual content, and more. This had profound implications for Nokia and marks the transition to a third phase.

While the Finnish mobile phone company had benefitted from a "first-mover advantage" in the late 1990s and early 2000s, this advantage was lost with the increasing dominance of smartphones. Smartphones provided online access and were therefore able to transfer pictures and video, display maps, and play music and radio. Not least, Nokia's setback was a result of Apple's launch of the first iPhone in 2007, which made the US company the market leader. Nokia's fall is illustrated by the company's decline from 5th place in 2009 to 57th place in 2013 in Interbrand's ranking of global brands

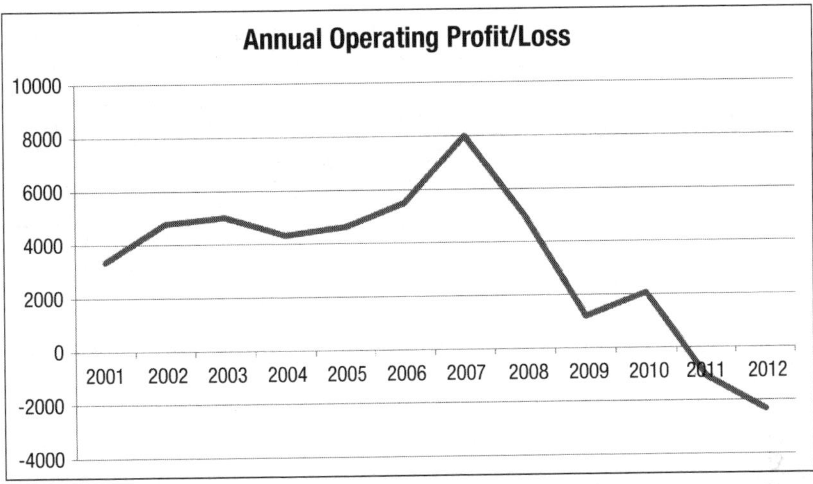

Fig. 5.2. Nokia Group: Annual profit/loss 2001–12 in million Euros. (Data from Nokia Group, 2003, 2004, 2005, 2006, 2007, 2008, 2009, 2010, 2011, 2012: data for years 2001–9.)

(Interbrand 2009, 2013), with figure 5.2 showing the dramatic decline in the company's annual profits since 2007.

As a result of the decline in sales and brand recognition, Nokia has sought to regain its dominant market position by expanding its product line and by mergers with the mobile and communication technology companies Siemens and Microsoft (Nokia 2011, 2013a). As a result of these mergers, the ownership of Nokia gradually became more international, until Nokia sold its Devices & Services division, responsible for the production of mobile phones as well as licenses to patents, to Microsoft in the autumn of 2013 (Nokia 2013b).

The Collaborative Company

We have pointed to Nokia as an example of a company that embodies collaboration. Important for the company's success is collaboration with the state and other operators, as well as a collaborative leadership style. Nokia has benefitted from cooperation with state bodies in Finland and also from Nordic cooperation. Four indications of collaboration are discussed here.

First, Nokia benefitted greatly from the large-scale telecom collaboration between the Nordic countries. In 1969, the Nordic Mobile Telephone Group, consisting of Sweden, Norway, and Denmark, was established with the aim of developing a new Pan-Nordic mobile telephone system (Steinbock 2003). The initiative came from Sweden, which at the time was a leading force in telecommunications, largely due to the technological innovations of its flagship company Ericsson (Castells and Himanen 2002, 55). In 1981 the Nordic Mobile Telephone network (NMT) was launched, becoming the world's first international cellular-telephone network standard and the first to allow international roaming, which caught on quickly across the world.

The introduction of the NMT standard was a precondition for the international success of the Nordic mobile phone industry, which expanded rapidly (Nokia 2013a). The new standard illustrates the characteristic collaboration between public and private stakeholders in telecom, a form of collaboration that was also open to ideas from equipment manufacturers such as Nokia (Castells and Himanen 2002, 55, 61).

The next step, the common European Standard for Mobile Communications (GSM), also began in the Nordic countries with a 1991 innovation by the Finnish company Radiolinja (Castells and Himanen 2002, 56). The introduction of a common technical standard within the European Union led the telecom sector into a phase of fierce competition (Steinbock 2010; Thussu 2006), as Nokia and other Nordic companies strategically made their products compatible with the new standard (Moen and Lilja 2005, 361). As a result, both Nokia and Ericsson suddenly found themselves among the top tier of international players with a "first-mover advantage"—competing with companies such as Motorola, Siemens, and Mitsubishi (Castells and Himanen 2002, 56). In 2001, the two main Nordic companies stood out due to their rapid overseas expansion and their soaring overseas revenue share of 97–98 percent (Steinbock 2003, 224). Nokia, along with other operators, had benefitted greatly from the Nordic collaborative move.

Second, Nokia has benefitted substantially in terms of both direct grants from and cooperation with the state. The Nordic states also remained key players in telecommunication after liberalization, while state involvement in the form of ownership, investments, and cooperation resulted in competitive market positions for Nordic telecom and associated companies. For Nokia, the Finnish National Technology Agency (TEKES) represented a key source of public funding for its research and development activities, and in the early 1980s, as much as 25 percent of Nokia's development costs were financed by the agency. The agency increased Nokia's ability to fund the development of analogue mobile communications (NMT) (Steinbock 2004, 57). Additionally, as Castells and Himanen point out, in the 1990s and the early part of the 2000s, the liberal regulatory environment and the collaboration with universities represented key factors in understanding the contribution of the public sector to Nokia's success (2002, 61).

A third indication of collaboration concerns the strategic mode of the company. Nokia relied on industry contract producers and partners, forming so-called collaborative systems in production and innovation (Moen and Lilja 2005, 362). With close partnerships with suppliers, and having partners with first-rate technical skills, Nokia could focus on its core areas (Moen and Lilja 2005, 362). As Nokia prepared for the launch of third generation mobile telecom (3G) in the late 1990s, such collaboration also came to include research and development and software development (Moen and Lilja 2005, 363; see Ali-Yrkkö 2001, 46–47). Nokia encouraged collaboration across the entire innovation chain, and the company became "an engine for the globalization of the emerging ICT sector of Finland" (Moen and Lilja 2005, 363).

Fourth and last, Nokia also emphasized collaboration within the company. Some argue that the Nokia executives' preoccupation with teamwork can be explained by the strong egalitarianism that characterizes Finnish society (Steinbock 2010, 41–42). The focus on the company's executive team rather than on Nokia's CEO differed from the focus of other multinational companies and very strongly from the personal mogul style of Stenbeck discussed earlier. In 1998, as Nokia expanded worldwide, *Business Week* magazine wrote a profile of Jorma Ollila, Nokia's CEO, and Ollila drew attention to the relationship between the company's leadership style and Finnish cultural norms: "We want to stress the team effort," and "I don't want to personalize Nokia with me. [Grandstanding] is not very Finnish, it's not very Nokia" (Ollila in *Business Week*, cited in Steinbock 2010, 41).

As we have shown, Nokia has benefitted from collaboration and cooperation on many levels. The company has collaborated extensively with other companies and the state, receiving direct funding and benefitting from publicly led technological advances. In turn, this provided Nokia with the opportunity for first-mover advantages and propelled the Finnish company into a global brand.

Summary

The study of the media companies Schibsted, the Modern Times Group, and Nokia aims to give a greater understanding of the role of private firms within the Nordic media and communications market. The chapter has discussed the companies' historical role and position, as well as their business strategies and management style. A focus has been put on understanding how these commercial firms relate to the Media Welfare State and particularly the fourth pillar: the tendency toward consensual and cooperative solutions between the main stakeholders.

In conclusion, we wish to highlight three observations:

First, there are a number of similarities between the expansion strategies of the three companies. All three companies have built on their strength in home markets and have gained economic, and in some cases cultural and political, capital to use as a basis for later expansion. Schibsted has benefitted from its protected national position and has gained economic leeway and public legitimacy, in addition to sustaining its role as a national cornerstone institution. In a similar way, Nokia benefitted greatly from direct public support for research and development and also from large-scale Nordic partnership in telecommunications. The Modern Times Group has not benefitted from direct state support, protection, or collaboration. Indirectly, though, the setup of the Nordic Media Welfare State represented a "green market" that the company exploited, and the restrictive Nordic media markets represented golden investment opportunities for the risk-taking Modern Times Group.

Second, the three companies also exemplify a typology of different strategies. Schibsted is expansionist, but simultaneously careful, and aims to avoid confrontations with regulators. Schibsted's executives publicly promote their views and argue that what is good for Schibsted is good for the Norwegian public and the principle of free speech. The company wishes to protect its role as a national cornerstone institution, while at the same time fighting for good market conditions, which is a careful balancing act. Nokia's development has been even more closely connected to the state through direct involvement and collaboration. Nokia earned first-mover advantage in telecommunications as a result of substantial public involvement, and a range of collaborative and private-public alliances made the Finnish company robust and flexible. Moreover, the collaborative culture also extends within the organization. In contrast to both Schibsted's adaptive strategy and Nokia's collaborative strategy, the Modern Times Group has chosen a confrontational style. The successes of its products and services have depended on a willingness to confront the established framework, and in cases such as that of Comvik and TV3, the company's well-timed launches led to important changes in both telecommunications and broadcasting.

Third, there are both similarities and differences in the ways that the companies have expanded internationally. A feature that Schibsted, the Modern Times Group, and Nokia all share is that their ability to expand internationally is partly based on the experience gained from launching businesses in the Nordic markets. The Modern Times Group achieved first-mover advantages in the market for commercial satellite television in Scandinavia, both as a content producer and as a broadcast distributor (Andersson 2000). Schibsted developed its newspaper business and the online classified service Finn.no in Norway before expanding internationally, whereas Nokia expanded outside Finland after achieving a major position in the home country. The three companies' similar approaches to expansion underline that although their relationships with the Media Welfare State differ, they are all key players in the internationalization, as well as the institutionalization and commercialization, of Nordic media.

// SIX //

Conclusion

This book has introduced the Media Welfare State as a concept connecting media systems with the Nordic model of society. The concept is based on analyses of media use, press structure, public service broadcasting, and commercial media and communications companies within the Nordic countries. In addition to our own analyses, we have based our understanding of the Media Welfare State on literature covering Nordic media. The Media Welfare State refers to principles that are more durable and consistent than specific regulatory measures and that influence media and communications across sectors and historical periods.

Through studies of the historical development of Nordic media, we found that four principles in particular were overarching and durable, labelling these the pillars of the Media Welfare State. The first pillar is a preference for organizing vital communication services in a way that underscores their character as public goods, with extensive cross-subsidies and obligations toward universality. The second pillar is a range of measures used to institutionalize freedom from editorial interference and self-governance in day-to-day operations of the media. Third, we identified a pillar of cultural policy that extends to the media in the form of content obligations and support schemes, aiming to secure diversity and quality. The last pillar is the preference for consensual solutions that are durable and involve cooperation between the main stakeholders: the state, communications industries, and the public (see table 1.1 and the appendix).

The studies in this book demonstrate that the media systems of the Nordic countries develop and change, while retaining key features. The period we have analyzed can be roughly divided into four phases: from the late 19th and early 20th centuries with the establishment of universal services in telecommunication and broadcasting; in the 1950s, 1960s, and 1970s with an expanding public service monopoly, the decline in the party press, and the introduction of press support; through the 1980s and 1990s with deregulation and introduction of commercial public service broadcasting; and digital and convergent media services from the mid-1990s and onward. In every phase, we have discussed adjustments and renewals of the organizational principles that support the Media Welfare State, as well as pointing to the adaptability of policy principles and solutions in the face of new challenges.

In this conclusion, we synthesize our findings and discuss the applicability of the theoretical framework of the Media Welfare State. The conclusion is structured around three issues that correspond to the three main premises of the book. Following this introduction, part 1 is about *continuity*. In this part we discuss the premise that continuity is just as important as change in Nordic media and present evidence for continuity on both the level of policy principles and the level of empirical realities. Part 2 is about *change*. In this part we discuss how marketization, globalization, social fragmentation, and authoritarianism continue to pose dilemmas for institutions and policymakers and how these forces take new forms in the digital age. Facing these challenges requires that policy measures and principles be adapted yet again. Part 3 is about *the Nordic* as a unit of analysis. To what degree have our analyses supported the view that the similarities between the Nordic countries are more profound than the differences? Part 4 concludes the book with a short note on research, particularly on the use of the concept of *crisis* to describe the current transformations in media and communications systems.

Continuity and Adaptability

Media studies, and particularly media policy studies, tend to be more interested in change than stability. One key premise of the book is that the interest in *continuity* should be stronger within media studies. It is therefore of course important to study change, but without a parallel emphasis on continuity the results may well be skewed. Generally speaking, studies of continuity will enrich the field of media research and pave the way for more interdisciplinary studies; what are the stabilizing factors across sectors and institutions? Specifically, as we stated in chapter 1, we wished to test the argument that continuity is just as important as change within Nordic media in the digital age.

As we have studied it in the book, continuity can be summarized on two levels: the level of organizational or policy principles and the level of empirical realities. We argue that although concrete ways of making policy and organizing media are modified and changed, the principles and practices that guide policy are to a large degree reaffirmed, sustained, and strengthened in the digital age. We further argue that there is a high degree of continuity regarding the empirical realities of how the media systems operate, whether we are speaking of user patterns, institutions, or content.

Beginning with the principles or pillars, we have shown in the book that *universalism* is a continuous principle in media policy-making. In our discussion of welfare state models in chapter 1, we pointed to universalism as a distinctive feature of Nordic welfare states from the very beginning—welfare provisions were set up not just as passive safety nets for the poor, but as a universal, high quality provision for all (Andersen et al. 2007; Esping-Andersen 1990). Universal access and a broad appeal have characterized Nordic media throughout their history, and the principle is strongly reaffirmed with the commitment to universal access to digital infrastructure (chap. 2).

There is also continuity regarding the principle of *editorial freedom*, which is described as the second pillar of the Media Welfare State. The long history of institutionalized press freedom—a freedom that is being respected—has been emphasized as a key characteristic of Nordic media (chaps. 3 and 4). This principle has been reaffirmed and extended to online media, in the sense that the mandate of the self-governing bodies and regulations has been extended. The connection between the first and second pillars is also discussed in the book. The concept of the socio-democratic information culture (Maier-Rabler 2008) links the principle of freedom of information with universal access to information and means of communication and sees both as preconditions for a working democracy.

Media policy has changed over the last decade, and economic and industrial policy goals have become more important, yet in the book we have shown the continued significance of *cultural policy goals*, the third pillar. Media and communications are still seen as vehicles to foster democratic and cultural involvement and participation, in addition to policy measures that aim to ensure that quality and diversity remain in place. Although their significance is reduced, press subsidies that aim to secure diversity in national, regional, and local press remain important parts of media regulation regimes (see chap. 3). Public service broadcasters continue to have strong political support, are granted a liberal regulatory framework, and continue to be obliged to promote national culture, as well as quality and diversity in output (see chap. 4).

Fourth, there is a continued tradition of *cooperative and consensual policy-making*. Consensual and cooperative policies have been important for turning Nordic countries into advanced information societies with high penetration and access to digital infrastructure, and there has been a shared commitment by all relevant stakeholders, both public and private, to actively use information and communication technology.

Even so, the fact that there is strong evidence of cooperation between public and private interests does not imply that frictions and conflicts are absent. Instead, our analyses have shown that concrete policy measures, such as the license fee and press support, are contested in some of the Nordic countries. Moreover, the discussions of media companies in chapter 5 illuminated how commercial enterprises have a dual relationship with the principles of the Media Welfare State: in many instances, the companies benefit from the cooperative traditions but are also constrained by them, and as we have shown, some companies have openly confronted the collaborative principle.

Although specific policy measures are contested, our contention is that the overarching pillars remain important for guiding policy in the digital age. This argument is supported with empirical analyses, in which we find substantial evidence for continuity in the use, content, and operation of media and communication services.

A first key finding in the book is the continuity *in user patterns*. In chapter 2 we argued that media use in the Nordic region has been egalitarian, albeit with relatively small differences between societal groups, and with major overlaps in the use of specific media. Our analyses showed that such patterns remain important in the digital age. While the region ranks high on the indexes of information and communication technology penetration and use, and while the inhabitants across the Nordic countries are comparatively heavy users of online media, to a large extent the uses come across as a continuation of traditional patterns. More specifically, there is continuity in the high interest in news and information, both in offline and online versions.

Second, the empirical analysis has demonstrated a continued *diversity in content*. Overall, there has been strong development toward more entertainment in all media windows and outlets. Nonetheless, we have discussed how a large number of newspapers continue to present a great diversity of views—locally, regionally, and nationally—and how the content of public service broadcasters continues to be significantly more diverse than that of commercial counterparts. Furthermore, we have argued that a high degree of diversity continues in the digital age, seen, for example, in the way that public service broadcasters venture into new media and experiment with multiplatform production (chap. 4). Partly as a result of these expansions diversity is upheld in an online environment, because rather than undermining traditional forms of output, the new channels for information and news distribution expand and complement existing output.

A third item of empirical evidence for continuity in Nordic media is that *traditional institutions remain strong*. The public service broadcasters in all Nordic countries continue to occupy a central position and maintain authority as *the* national broadcasters, and they have a strong online presence (chap. 4). Traditional newspaper publishers have a strong presence in new media and have found ways to incorporate online journalism into existing practices. As demonstrated in chapter 5, key national media institutions have successfully adjusted their strategies to digital and global markets. For example, the Norwegian publisher Schibsted has expanded from a national and pan-Nordic newspaper company into a large international conglomerate with a strong position in publishing and online classifieds (chaps. 3 and 5).

In sum, the book has pinpointed areas of continuity in media use, content, and institutions. Media companies tend to follow well-trodden paths confronted with new challenges, and user preferences do not change overnight. What we have also aimed to illustrate in the book, as well as in this summary, is the strong connection between continuity and adaptability. Continuity does not mean the absence of change, but rather that strategies and measures are adapted to new realities—within the framework of durable principles.

Importantly, the adaptability in the cited cases is not one-sided: it is not only the users and companies that adapt—regulators and the state also do so, partly facilitating the changes. While the strong influence of the state is often thought of as a distinguishing characteristic of Nordic media, we have argued that just as important is the Nordic states' pragmatic relationship with private businesses and the ability to reform through a public-private mix. In many ways the role of the state comes more into focus in the digital age—not only as a regulator but also as a facilitator—which stands out as an important object of study for media scholars.

In the years following the liberalization of telecommunication and broadcasting in the 1980s and 1990s, the emphasis in scholarship and debate was on the withdrawal of the state from traditional areas of regulation, though more recently this has been corrected with an increased scholarly focus on "The return of the state" (Jessop 2010; Grewald 2010; ICA 2013). An important question in the digital era is how state measures are modified and transformed yet again to handle new problems and challenges.

Regulatory Dilemmas in the Digital Age

Media policy does not appear out of nowhere, but is instigated in response to problems—whether real or perceived. In the book, we have argued that four forces in particular—marketization, globalization, social fragmentation, and authoritarianism—create problems, which in turn have triggered political intervention in the media system. These forces persist in the digital era and also occur in new forms. Responding to them requires ingenuity and creativity on the part of policymakers and institutions, namely: how to adapt and transform strategies and policy measures developed in the analogue era to be effective in a new situation? The question concerns how to instigate *change*, while retaining key features crucial to the public interest.

In this part, we begin with some illustrative dilemmas under the heading of *marketization*. The adoption of market principles in new areas has influenced policies, media systems, and the production and distribution of media content. We have seen how Nordic media companies have exploited new market opportunities and expanded both inside and outside the region and how audiences have been given a greater choice and opportunities for media use. However, we have also pointed out how marketization potentially challenges the policy goals of the Media Welfare State. For example, the attention to profitable niche markets may induce digital gaps, and quality may spiral downward when media content is recycled on many platforms.

The perhaps most difficult dilemma associated with marketization is the question of how to fund journalism. Existing and traditional business models for journalism are under quite extensive pressure in the digital era (see chap. 3). Traditionally, funding models for media have relied on the media as a mixed suite of content in which the revenue collected pays for the entire package. With digitalization and convergence, this system is dissolving in both the press and broadcasting. We see a decoupling of advertising and editorial content, a decline in the sales of printed newspapers, and an intensified competition for advertising revenue from new actors who do not produce journalistic content (such as Facebook, Google, and LinkedIn). In broadcasting, the dissemination of content across multiple platforms blurs the line between public and commercial funding. In both publishing and broadcasting, a key issue for policymakers is how to adapt the policy measures in which public funding plays a part. Public support mechanisms such as the license fee and press subsidies are not easily transferred to the online environment, and they are also challenged and seen to distort competition by companies who do not qualify for state support.

From a historical perspective, a range of measures has been implemented to modify the impact of *standardization and globalization*. The Nordic public service broadcasters have been regarded in particular as vehicles of cultural defense, whereas the political intention to protect national culture and language has also legitimized policy measures in publishing, commercial broadcasting, and other media. With the emergence of conglomerates that operate both globally and in national markets, the demarcation lines between the national and international levels become more blurred. As Nordic media institutions enter the online media market, the services they offer are frequently related to expanding international players such as Google, Twitter, and Facebook. This provides opportunities for connecting with users in new ways, but also brings the institutions into a territory of difficult ethical, financial, and editorial questions. For example, the influence of Facebook is considerable, not least in the way that the social media network has become a communications infrastructure in its own right. The presence of expanding, global players residing outside national borders, without any formal or regulatory relationships with Nordic governments, further challenges traditional methods of consensus-building and collaboration between public and private interests. The international players press for standardized regulatory frameworks that function in the same way across national settings and do not take part in the traditional forms of dialogue such as public hearings, formal and informal meetings, and open public debate.

A range of policy measures to combat *social fragmentation* has also been instigated in the Nordic countries, and in the book we have discussed the moderate class, gender, and ethnic differences. Moreover, both social structures and media user patterns have been egalitarian, and the Nordic populations have been culturally homogenous. Recently, two parallel developments have imposed changes: On the one hand, media output is becoming increasingly fragmented, not least through the endless choices and niche services offered by the Internet economy (Anderson 2006; Turow 2011). On the other hand, the Nordic population is becoming more pluralistic, both in the sense of being ethnically and culturally more mixed and because of a liberal information regime that allows a wide variety of perspectives to be expressed (chap. 2).

The Nordic liberal information regime, particularly in light of the increased social fragmentation, poses dilemmas for both institutions and regulators. Perhaps the most acute challenge for media institutions is how to control politically extremist expressions, especially in online debates and user-generated content. In the aftermath of the July 22, 2011, terrorist attack in Norway, which we have cited as a case in several chapters, questions have been raised regarding the need to protect society and individuals from threats and hateful content on the Internet. While the editorial strategy in some media has been to prohibit anonymous posts and intensify monitoring in online debates, there has essentially been no tightening of speech. States are usually criticized for overreacting to terrorism (e.g., Freedman 2008), but in a Nordic context the question that is publicly debated is whether online extremism is treated too lightly. While the dominant view is that the repression of speech produces intensified extremism and polarization, others claim that the opposite is the case. For example, the Norwegian philosopher Lene Auestad argues that after the terrorist attack in 2011, hate speech has actually become more visible in the Norwegian debate and argues that "by accepting the presence of hate speech we are changing the norms for what is acceptable to say" (Auestad cited in Simonnes 2013, authors' translation). For regulators committed to media self-governance, the pressing question becomes how to respond adequately to hateful and extremist expressions, as well as how to secure the rights of minorities and safeguard the rights of all citizens.

A related dilemma can be discussed under the heading of *authoritarianism*. In the 19th and 20th centuries, Nordic policymakers and publishers explicitly rejected the idea of state-controlled media as a part of an antiauthoritarian struggle. From the Enlightenment onward, there was a struggle for rational debate and against the power of the Crown and Church, and a liberal climate gradually evolved in which just about everything was allowed in terms of the criticism of magistrates, religious dogma, and other people's beliefs. However, the combination of digitalization, convergence, and globalization makes the Nordic liberal publishing approaches, in addition to the openness in the socio-democratic information culture, more contested and complicated.

In the book, we have discussed the controversy around the Danish newspaper *Jyllands-Posten*'s editorial decision to publish the Mohammed cartoon drawings in 2005. The publication triggered protests and a political and diplomatic crisis between the Nordic region and several Muslim countries, particularly affecting Denmark. The conflict demonstrates how editorial decisions and traditions may be accepted and understood by stakeholders and long-term residents of one country, but may not be accepted by new residents, as well as readers, listeners, and viewers in other parts of the world. The different ideals of press freedom have traditionally been part of separate national media spheres, but as a result of recent trends of globalization and digitalization, these spheres have increasingly merged. In the wake of the cartoon controversy, several of the fundamental premises of the liberal information regime were contested: it was demanded that the Nordic governments should discipline the media in question, otherwise they would be treated as being co-responsible; and it was demanded of the media that they respect religious dogmas. As different ideals of press and editorial freedom clash in the digital media landscape, a significant question is how to balance the mechanisms that legitimize such freedoms and those that challenge them.

How Nordic Is the Media Welfare State?

Rather than studying and comparing each national system, this book has approached the Nordic area as one region. This approach is based on the evidence of a great similarity across the Nordic countries. Still, this type of unified Nordic approach is not very common. In this part of the conclusion, we recapitulate evidence of national differences and similarities and pose the question: how *Nordic* are the characteristics we have detected?

Identifying the Nordic region as a special case requires support on two interrelated counts: the cases must be internally similar, and as a group they must diverge from other countries and regions. We have argued in the book that both conditions are met. However, this neither means that the Nordic countries are identical, nor that the features of Nordic media and communications are unique to the region.

Many studies point to differences between the Nordic countries' media and communication systems, and there is also a tendency to criticize general models such as Hallin and Mancini's (2004) for masking important national differences (Nord 2008; Strömbäck, Ørsten and Aalberg 2008; Kjær and Slaatta 2007; Nieminen 2013).

We agree that there are substantial and important differences within the Nordic region and have pointed to several in the preceding chapters. Compared to the other Nordic countries, for example, the Finns are less ardent cinemagoers, the Danes watch more television, the Swedes read less online news, and the Icelanders upload more of their own content online (chap. 2). Denmark and Iceland have fewer titles and fewer local papers, Norway does not have a tradition of free newspapers, and the system of press support is nowadays more marginalized in Finland than elsewhere in the Nordic region (chap. 3). In Iceland, the license fee for public service broadcasting was abolished in 2007, and the public service broadcaster, RÚV, also takes advertising. Finland has recently switched from a license fee to a broadcast tax, whereas in Denmark the license fee has been extended to online media terminals.

In the book, we have further acknowledged that the choice of methodology may disguise relevant variations (chap. 1). In several instances, we have had to base our observations on data that do not cover all the Nordic countries. To provide more depth, we have illustrated the discussion with cases from individual countries, which are not chosen as being representative, and it is also true that the distinct features of the smallest Nordic country, Iceland, do not play a large part in the book.

Despite these findings and shortcomings, our contention is that a Nordic perspective can provide new insights, both empirically and theoretically. Media structures, institutions, and user patterns display a set of common traits across national boundaries that are worth both exploring and explaining, and it seems that that national differences are more significant in specific policy measures than in overarching principles and empirical realities. Viewed from an international perspective, Nordic countries cluster on a number of indicators related to social *outcomes*—such as the degree of happiness, social trust, freedom of speech, leverage of information and communication technologies, and patterns of media use. In sum, this clustering emerges as a distinct pattern when the Nordic countries are compared with other countries and regions.

This leads us to the second part of the question: To what degree do the Nordic traits differ from those of other countries and regions? Through studies of media use, the press, public service broadcasting, and media companies we have shown that there are indeed a number of features where the Nordic patterns are similar to those of other countries.

For instance, chapter 3 showed that continental European countries appear on the top of press-freedom rankings together with the Nordic countries and that press freedom characterizes the Netherlands and Switzerland no less perhaps than Sweden, Norway, Denmark, Finland, and Iceland. Many aspects of the media structure and media use in the Nordic countries correspond with the structures and use in countries with similar societal models. Not surprisingly, we find many similarities between the media organization and user patterns in the Nordic countries and in other countries classified as corporatist or social-democratic (chaps. 1 and 2).

However, it is interesting that the similarities with other countries are not consistent, but depend on which elements of the media system we are observing. In the book, we have also shown that in some respects Nordic media and communication patterns and institutions resemble those of very different systems. For example, in many ways, the Nordic structures of public service broadcasting are similar to those of the United Kingdom and Japan. Moreover, we have referred to surveys in which the digital communication infrastructures in the Nordic countries bear similarities to those of Luxembourg, Korea, Hong Kong, Singapore, Canada, and the United States.

Consequently, our conclusion is similar to the conclusions that emerge in studies of welfare state variations: the Nordic countries have much in common with similarly wealthy Western societies, but have more in common with each other (Andersen et al. 2007, 14). To the degree that one can speak at all of regional media and communications structures, Nordic media constitute a distinct entity.

The Nordic countries cooperate extensively and have in many instances actively coordinated specific media policy measures. Yet, there is a certain taken-for-granted attitude to Nordic cooperation, and Nordic media managers and policymakers seem more inspired by developments elsewhere. For Nordic media companies, a key source of inspiration is the United States, a leading country in media innovation that hosts several of the largest enterprises in current global media markets (see chap. 5). For further research it is interesting to ask to what degree developments in the Nordic countries will remain synchronous and which of other countries' media systems will develop along similar lines. In order to answer such questions, there is a need not only to compare the Nordic countries with other Western countries, but also to compare their media systems with systems beyond the West (e.g., Dobek-Ostrowska et al. 2010; Hallin and Mancini 2012a).

Crisis—a Final Note

In the study of media and communications, and not least in media policy studies, there is an emphasis on upheaval and disruption. The concept of crisis is often used—both in the public debate and in scholarship—to describe how traditional institutions of media and communications are threatened by forces such as marketization and globalization. Studies of public service broadcasting have been informed by a "crisis discourse" for several decades (chap. 4), it has been commonplace to talk about a "crisis" in the newspaper industry (chap. 3), and there is a sense of crisis in the discussions over the fragmentation of the public sphere (chap. 2).

The concept of crisis is used in the public debate, but is also much referred to in media scholarship. We have ourselves used this and similar concepts (see, e.g., Syvertsen 1991; Moe 2003), yet we remain unsure of whether this is a fruitful term.

One reason for this is that the concept is rarely defined very precisely. The concept of crisis is often used rhetorically by media actors to, for example, mobilize public support for political intervention, subsidy, and protection, which requires a certain analytical distance on the part of researchers. Furthermore, there is a danger that dramatic concepts of this nature may mask how change is a normal aspect of media development, as forms of content, economic models, or modes of communication emerge and fade over time. The focus on dramatic upheavals may mask how changes occur to a different degree and at a different pace in different parts of the world.

Perhaps the most important reason why dramatic concepts should be avoided in studies of media change is that such concepts mask the possibilities for action. Crises are often understood as a form of structural breakdown, and the use of such terms downplays how different actors willfully choose different solutions and pursue different goals. We have shown how media companies have pressed for political change and in various ways taken advantage of new possibilities for profit, but also how such companies may be committed to nonprofit goals (chap. 5). An important argument of this book is that policy makers and institutions are resourceful, resilient, and adaptable to changing circumstances. Rather than a dramatic break with the past, there are a number of microdecisions that transform media and communications, as well as many possibilities for managing and reorienting both policymaking and strategy.

In this book, we have done empirical studies on media use, the press, broadcasting, and private companies. Theoretically, we found combining studies from political science and sociology with perspectives from media studies rewarding, as it enabled us to identify a set of similarities between the societal characteristics and the principles and practices of media policymaking. Nonetheless, the approach and the concept of the Media Welfare State remain tentative and need further elaboration and investigation.

Appendix. The Four Pillars of the Media Welfare State—Extended Version

Pillars	Media Use	Press	Broadcasting	Company
1: An organization of vital communication services that underscores their character as *public goods,* with extensive cross-subsidies and obligations toward universality	Media user patterns are characterized by egalitarianism and commonality. Media user patterns are shaped by the commitment to universal Internet and broadband access.	Egalitarian readership is based on universal education, small class and gender differences. Content is based on egalitarian ideals, less of an elite/mass distinction.	Broadcasting is conceived as a public good. Equal access for citizens to well-funded radio and television Equal payment by citizens through public funding/license fee	Private media and communications companies are key players in the institutionalization, commercialization, and internationalization of Nordic media. These companies produce affordable communications hardware and popularize digital content and services. They promote segmentation, but their press operations are to a large extent based on egalitarian ideals.
2: A range of measures used to institutionalize *freedom from editorial interference* and self-governance in day-to-day operations	Universal access to Internet rooted in socio-democratic information culture, where access to information is seen as a basic right	Press freedom was introduced early. The level of press freedom is comparatively very high. Well-functioning self-regulation	Editorial freedom granted to public service broadcasters License fee funding to secure independence from the state and the market	Private media and communications companies enjoy editorial freedom and in some cases promote press freedom internationally.
3: A *cultural policy that extends to the media* in the form of content obligations and support schemes that aim to secure diversity and quality	Equal access to information is a key policy to foster democracy. Media and communications are seen as vehicles to enhance democratic and cultural involvement and participation.	Press support is an example of cultural policy extended to the media. Press support aims to sustain diversity of the press.	Public service broadcasters are seen as vehicles for enlightenment and democracy. They are obliged to promote national culture, quality, and diversity in output. Some private broadcasters have similar obligations.	Private media and communications companies benefit from cultural policies, but have also been constrained by them and in some cases openly confronted them.

Pillars	Media Use	Press	Broadcasting	Company
4: A preference for consensual solutions that are durable and involve *cooperation between main stakeholders:* the state, the media and communications industries, and the public.	Consensual and cooperative policies are key to turning the Nordic countries into advanced information societies with high levels of penetration and access. Commitment to use ICT by all stakeholders.	Press policy is a classic example of the public-private mix. Private newspapers are seen as important for democracy and they benefit from supportive policies.	Public service broadcasters were established as compromise solutions, but have evolved into popular institutions with high legitimacy, but not all stakeholders support public funding.	Private media and communication companies exemplify the private-public mix, but their relation to collaborative traditions varies from adapting to them to opposing them.

References

Ala-Fossi, Marko. 2012. "Social Obsolescence of the TV Fee and the Financial Crisis of Finnish Public Service Media." *Journal of Media Business Studies* 9 (1): 33–54.

Alestalo, Matti, Sven E. O. Hort, and Stein Kuhnle. 2009. "The Nordic Model: Conditions, Origins, Outcomes, Lessons." Hertie School of Governance Working Paper No. 41. June.

Alexa.com. 2012. "The Top 500 Sites in Each Country or Territory." http://www.alexa.com/topsites/countries. Accessed October 13, 2012.

Ali-Yrkkö, Jyrki. 2001. *Nokia's Network—Gaining Competitiveness from Co-operation*. ETLA B-174. The Research Institute of the Finnish Economy. Helsinki: Taloustieto Oy.

Allern, Sigurd, and Mark Blach-Ørsten. 2011. "The News Media as a Political Institution: A Scandinavian Perspective." *Journalism Studies* 12 (1): 92–105.

Andersen, Torben M. 2008a. "The Nordic Welfare Model—Flavour of the Month?" In *Copyright Norden. The Nordic Model—Fact or Fiction?*, edited by Jesper Schou-Knudsen, 11–19. Copenhagen: Nordic Council and Nordic Council of Ministers.

Andersen, Torben M. 2008b. "The Scandinavian Model—Prospects and Challenges." *International Tax and Public Finance* 15 (1): 45–66.

Andersen, Torben M., Bengt Holmström, Seppo Honkapohja, Sixten Korkman, Hans Tson Söderström, and Juhana Vartiainen. 2007. *The Nordic Model. Embracing Globalization and Sharing Risks*. ETLA B232. The Research Institute of the Finnish Economy. Helsinki: Taloustieto Oy.

Anderson, Benedict. 1992. *Imagined Communities: Reflections on the Origin and Spread of Nationalism*. London: Verso.

Anderson, Chris. 2006. *The Long Tail: Why the Future of Business Is Selling Less of More*. New York: Hyperion.

Andersson, Jonas. 2009. "For the Good of the Net: The Pirate Bay as a Strategic Sovereign." *Culture Machine* 10:64–108.

Andersson, Per. 2000. *Stenbeck. En reportage om det virtuella bruket*. Stockholm: Norsteds.

Ásgrímsson, Halldór, and Jan-Erik Enestam. 2008. "Foreword." In *Copyright Norden. The Nordic Model—Fact or Fiction?*, edited by Jesper Schou-Knudsen and the Nordic Council of Ministers' Communication Department, 5. Copenhagen: Nordic Council and Nordic Council of Ministers.

Aslama, Minna, and Trine Syvertsen. 2007. "Public Service Broadcasting and New Technologies: Marginalisation or Re-Monopolisation." In *Media between Culture and Commerce*, edited by Els De Bens, 167–78. Bristol: Intellect.

Barland, Jens. 2005. "Press Freedom and Globalisation: Scandinavia and East Africa Compared." Master thesis, United States International University, Nairobi, Kenya.

Barland, Jens. 2012. "Journalistikk for markedet. Redaksjonell produktutvikling i VG og Aftonbladet på papir og nett 1995–2010." PhD diss., University of Oslo.

Bastiansen, Henrik G. 1991. "'Herr Kringkastingssjef!'—Et seerperspektiv på innføringen av fjernsynet i Norge 1960–1963." In *Om filmimport, seerbrev, kilder og 60-åra*, Levende bilder no. 3, edited by Kathrine Skretting, 9–60. Oslo and Trondheim: NAVF.

Bastiansen, Henrik G. 1994. *Live from the Moon. En casestudie i fjernsynets historie*. Levende bilder no. 2. Oslo: Norges Forskningsråd.

Bastiansen, Henrik G., and Hans Fredrik Dahl. 2003. *Norsk Mediehistorie*. Oslo: Universitetsforlaget.

Bastiansen, Henrik G., and Hans Fredrik Dahl. 2008. *Norsk mediehistorie*, 2nd ed. Oslo: Universitetsforlaget.

Bastiansen, Henrik, and Trine Syvertsen. 1996. "Towards a Norwegian Television History." In *Television in Scandinavia: History, Politics and Aesthetics*, edited by Ib Bondebjerg and Francesco Bono, 127–55. Luton: John Libbey Media.

BBC. 2009. "Norway 'the Best Place to Live.'" http://news.bbc.co.uk/2/hi/in_depth/8290550.stm. Accessed February 15, 2013.

BBC. 2012. "Samsung Overtakes Nokia in Mobile Shipments." April 27. http://www.bbc.co.uk/news/business-17865117. Accessed October 31, 2013.

Bechman, Anja. 2010. "I leverer, vi præsenterer: Om underholdningsverdi I brugerproduceret TV." In *TV og underholdning*, edited by Kirsten Frandsen and Hanne Bruun. Århus: Aarhus Universitetsforlag.

Bell, Daniel. 1973. *The Coming of Post-Industrial Society*. Harmondsworth: Penguin.

Benkler, Yochai. 2006. *The Wealth of Networks: How Social Production Transforms Markets and Freedom*. New Haven, CT: Yale University Press.

Benson, Rodney. 2010. "Futures of the News: International Considerations and Further Reflections." In *New Media, Old News: Journalism and Democracy in the Digital Age*, edited by Natalie Fenton, 187–200. London: Sage.

Berg, Christian E., and Anker B. Lund. 2012. "Financing Public Service Broadcasting: A Comparative Perspective." *Journal of Media Business Studies* 9 (1): 7–22.

Blekesaune, Arild, Eiri Elvestad, and Toril Aalberg. 2012. "Tuning out the World of News and Current Affairs—An Empirical Study of Europe's Disconnected Citizens." *European Sociological Review*, 28(1): 110–26.

Blum, Roger. 2005. "Bausteine zu einer Theorie der Mediensysteme." *Medienwissenschaft Schweiz* 2: 5–11.

Bondebjerg, Ib. 1996. "Modern Danish Television–after the Monopoly Era." In *Television in Scandinavia: History, Politics and Aesthetics*, edited by Ib Bondebjerg and Francesco Bono, 41–69. Luton: University of Luton Press.

Bondebjerg, Ib, and Francesco Bono, eds. 1996. *Television in Scandinavia: History, Politics and Aesthetics*. Luton: University of Luton Press.

Born, Georgina. 2004. *Uncertain Vision: Birt, Dyke and the Reinvention of the BBC*. London: Secker & Warburg.

boyd, danah. 2007. "Why Youth (Heart) Social Network Sites: The Role of Networked Publics in Teenage Social Life." In *Youth, Identity, and Digital Media*, edited by David Buckingham, 119–42. Cambridge, MA: MIT Press. http://www.Danah.org/papers/WhyYouthHeart.pdf. Accessed October 3, 2011.

Brandtzæg, Petter B. 2012. "Social Implications of the Internet and Social Networking Sites: A User Typology Approach." PhD diss., University of Oslo.

Brants, Kees, and Denis McQuail. 1992. "The Netherlands." In *The Media in Western Eu-*

rope. *The Euromedia Handbook*, 2nd ed., edited by Bernt Østergaard, 144–67. London: Sage.

Brevini, Benedetta. 2010. "Towards PSB 2.0? Applying the PSB Ethos to Online Media in Europe: A Comparative Study of PSBs' Internet Policies in Spain, Italy and Britain." *European Journal of Communication* 25 (4): 348–65.

Brown, Allan, and Robert G. Picard, eds. 2004. *Digital Terrestrial Television in Europe*. London: Lawrence Erlbaum.

Brügger, Niels. 2012. "The Idea of Public Service in the Early History of DR Online." In *Histories of Public Service Broadcasters on the Web*, edited by Maureen Burns and Niels Brügger, 91–104. New York: Peter Lang.

Bruun, Hanne. 2005. "Public Service and Entertainment. A Case Study of Danish Television 1951–2003." In *Cultural Dilemmas in Public Service Broadcasting—Ripe@2005*, edited by Gregory Ferrell Lowe and Per Jauert, 143–63. Göteborg: Nordicom.

Bruun, Hanne. 2012. "Audience Constructions in Political Talk Shows." Paper presented at the the 4th European Communication Conference, ECREA. Istanbul, Turkey, October 24–27.

Carlsson, Ulla. 2010a. "Young People in the Digital Media Culture. Global and Nordic Perspectives—An Introduction." In *Children and Youth in the Digital Media Culture. From a Nordic Horizon*, edited by Ulla Carlsson, 9–22. Göteborg: Nordicom.

Carlsson, Ulla, ed. 2010b. "Nordicom-Sveriges Mediebarometer 2010." *MedieNotiser* Nr. 1, Göteborg: Nordicom, Göteborgs universitet.

Carlsson, Ulla, and Ulrika Facht, eds. 2010. *Mediesverige 2010. Statistik og analys*. Göteborg: Nordicom, Göteborgs universitet.

Castells, Manuel, and Pekka Himanen. 2002. *The Information Society and the Welfare State: The Finnish Model*. Oxford: Oxford University Press.

Cedergren, Herman S. 2007. "A Strategic Analysis of New Media's Influence on Schibsted and Orkla Media." Master's thesis, Norwegian School of Management.

Chapman, Jane. 2005. *Comparative Media History*. Malden, MA: Polity Press.

Christensen, Christian. 2011. "Discourses of Technology and Liberation: State Aid to Net Activists in an Era of 'Twitter Revolutions.'" *Communication Review* 14 (3): 233–53.

Christiansen, Niels Finn, and Pirjo Markkola. 2006. "Introduction." In *The Nordic Model of Welfare: A Historical Reappraisal*, edited by Niels Finn Christiansen, Klaus Petersen, Nils Edling, and Per Haave, 9–31. Copenhagen: Museum Tusculanum Press.

Christiansen, Niels Finn, Klaus Petersen, Nils Edling, and Per Haave, eds. 2006. *The Nordic Model of Welfare: A Historical Reappraisal*. Copenhagen: Museum Tusculanum Press.

Coleman, Stephen, and John Gøtze. 2001. *Bowling Together: Online Public Engagement in Policy Deliberation*. London: Hansard Society.

Conde, Anxo Lamela. 2008. "Myth, Reality and Challenges." In *Copyright Norden. The Nordic Model—Fact or Fiction?*, edited by Jesper Schou-Knudsen and the Nordic Council and Nordic Council of Ministers' Communications Department, 53–59. Copenhagen: Nordic Council and Nordic Council of Ministers.

Couldry, Nick. 2007. "Comparative Media Research as If We Really Meant It." *Global Media and Communication* 3 (3): 247–71.

Da, Lei. 2008. "The Nordic Model Is Not Suitable for China." In *Copyright Norden. The Nordic Model—Fact or Fiction?*, edited by Jesper Schou-Knudsen and the Nordic

Council and Nordic Council of Ministers' Communications Department, 65–71. Copenhagen: Nordic Council and Nordic Council of Ministers.

Dagbladet. 2010. "Rekordmange organdonasjoner." January 14. http://www.dagbladet.no/2010/01/14/tema/helse/organdonasjon/9923958/. Accessed February 25, 2013.

Dahl, Hans Fredrik. 2003. "Orkla mot Schibsted: Kampen om den norske TV2-konsesjonen." In *Pennan, Penningen & Politiken: Medier och medieföretag förr och nu*, edited by Ulla Carlsson, 183–96. Göteborg: Nordicom.

Dahl, Hans Fredrik, and Henrik G. Bastiansen. 1999. *Over til Oslo: NRK som monopol. 1945–1981*. Oslo: Cappelen.

Danmarks Statistik. 2011. *Befolkningens brug af Internet 2010*. København: Danmarks statistik.

D'Arma, Alessandro. 2010. "Italian Television in the Multichannel Age: Change and Continuity in Industry Structure, Programming and Consumption." *Convergence* 16 (2): 201–15.

D'Arma, Alessandro, Gunn Enli, and Jeanette Steemers. 2010. "Serving Children in Public Service Media." In *The Public in Public Service Media—Ripe@2009*, edited by Gregory Ferrell Lowe, 227–42. Göteborg: Nordicom.

Davidson, Roei, Nathaniel Poor, and Ann Williams. 2009. "Stratification and Global Elite Theory: A Cross-Cultural and Longitudinal Analysis of Public Opinion." *International Journal of Public Opinion Research* 21 (2): 165–86.

Davis, Gerald F. 2009. *Managed by the Markets: How Finance Re-shaped America*. New York: Oxford University Press.

Dayan, Daniel, and Elihu Katz. 1994. *Media Events: The Live Broadcasting of History*. Cambridge, MA: Harvard University Press.

De Bens, Els. 1992. "Belgium." In *The Media in Western Europe: The Euromedia Handbook*, 2nd ed., edited by Bernt Østergaard, 17–34. London: Sage.

Delhey, Jan, and Kenneth Newton. 2005. "Predicting Cross-National Levels of Social Trust: Global Pattern or Nordic Exceptionalism?" *European Sociological Review* 21 (4): 311–27.

Dobek-Ostrowska, Boguslawa, Michal Głowacki, Karol Jakubowicz, and Miklós Sükösd, eds. 2010. *Comparative Media Systems: European and Global Perspectives*. Budapest and NY: Central European University Press.

Donders, Karen, and Hallvard Moe, eds. 2011. *Exporting the Public Value Test: The Regulation of Public Broadcasters' New Media Services across Europe*. Göteborg: Nordicom.

Doyle, Gillian. 2013. *Understanding Media Economics*. 2nd ed. London: Sage.

Duelund, Peter. 2003. "The Nordic Cultural Model" In *The Nordic Cultural Model*, edited by Peter Duelund, 479–530. Copenhagen: Nordic Cultural Institute.

DR. 2012. http://www.dr.dk/NR/rdonlyres/A2833DC1-2A19-4FB9-8794-EC2DBA-5FA44C/3772295/resume2011.pdf. Accessed August 4, 2013.

Econ. 2008. "Nedlasting av film." *ECON-rapport* 2008–034. Oslo: Econ.

Economist Intelligence Unit. 2010. *Digital Economy Rankings 2010*. http://graphics.eiu.com/upload/EIU_Digital_economy_rankings_2010_FINAL_WEB.pdf. Accessed May 10, 2014.

Edin, Anna. 2000. *Den föreställda publiken: programpolitik, publikbilder och tiltalsformer i svensk public service-television*. Stockholm/Stehag: Brutus Östlings Bokförlag Symposion.

Egenfeldt-Nielsen, Simon. 2003. "Computerspil på skoleskemaet." *Berlingske Tidende*.

http://www.b.dk/din-mening/computerspil-paa-skoleskemaet. Accessed August 1, 2013.

Eide, Martin. 1999. "Pressen—institusjoner og historie." In *Medier—institusjoner og historie, Medievitenskap*, vol. 1, edited by Peter Larsen and Liv Hausken, 157–73. Bergen: Fagbokforlaget.

Eide, Martin. 2000. *Den Redigerende Makt. Redaktørrollens norske historie.* Kristiansand: IJ-forlaget.

Eide, Martin, ed. 2010. *En samfunnsmakt blir til 1660–1880, Norsk presses histoire*, vol. 1. Oslo: Universitetsforlaget.

Eide, Martin, Leif Ove Larsen, and Helle Sjøvaag, eds. 2012. *Nytt på nett og brett. Journalistikk i forandring.* Oslo: Universitetsforlaget.

Einhorn, Eric S., and John Logue. 2004. "Can the Scandinavian Model Adapt to Globalization?" *Scandinavian Studies* 76 (4): 501–34.

Elvestad, Eiri, and Arild Blekesaune. 2008. "Newspaper Readers in Europe. A Multilevel Study of Individual and National Differences." *European Journal of Communication* 23 (4): 425–47.

Engebretsen, Martin. 2006. "Shallow and Static or Deep and Dynamic? Studying the State of Online Journalism in Scandinavia." *Nordicom Review* 27 (1): 3–16.

Enjolras, Bernard, Kari Steen-Johnsen, and Dag Wollebæk. 2012. "Social Media and Mobiliziation to Offline Demonstrations: Transcending Participatory Divides?" *New Media & Society*, 1–19. Accessed February 15, 2013.

Enli, Gunn. 2008. "Redefining Public Service Broadcasting: Multiplatform Participation." *Convergence* 14 (1): 105–20.

Enli, Gunn. 2013. "Defending Nordic Children against Disney. PSB Children's Channels in the Age of Globalization." *Nordicom Review* 34 (1): 77–90.

Enli, Gunn, and Brian McNair. 2010. "Trans-National Reality TV: A Comparative Study of the U.K.'s and Norway's Wife Swap." In *Trans-Reality Television*, edited by Nico Carpentier and Sofie Van Bauwel, 205–77. Lanham: Lexington Books.

Enli, Gunn, Hallvard Moe, Vilde Schanke Sundet, and Trine Syvertsen. 2010. *TV—en innføring.* Oslo: Universitetsforlaget.

Enli, Gunn, and Eli Skogerbø. 2013. "Personalized Campaigns in Party-Centered Politics: Twitter and Facebook as Arenas for Political Communication." *Information, Communication & Society* 16 (5): 757–74.

Enli, Gunn, and Elisabeth Staksrud. 2013. "PSB Serving Children. Past, Present and Future." In *Public Service Media from a Nordic Horizon. Politics, Markets, Programming and Users*, edited by Ulla Carlsson, 117–30. Göteborg: Nordicom.

Enli, Gunn, and Vilde Schanke Sundet. 2007. "Strategies in Times of Regulatory Change: A Norwegian Case Study on the Battle for a Commercial Radio Licence." *Media, Culture & Society* 29 (5): 707–25.

Erdal, Ivar J. 2007. "Lokomotiver og sugerør: Om medieplattformenes roller i en allmennkringkasters nyhetsorganisasjon." In *På tværs af medierne*, edited by Anja Bechmann Petersen and Steen K. Rasmussen, 153–76. Århus: Forlaget Ajour.

Erikson, Robert, Erik Jørgen Hansen, Stein Ringen, and Hannu Uusitalo. 1987. *The Scandinavian Model: Welfare States and Welfare Research.* Armonk, NY: M. E. Sharpe.

Esping-Andersen, Gøsta. 1990. *The Three Worlds of Welfare Capitalism.* Princeton, NJ: Princeton University Press.

Esping-Andersen, Gøsta, ed. 1996. *Welfare States in Transition: National Adaptations in Global Economies*. London: Sage.

Eurostat. 2011. *Cultural Statistics, 2011 Edition: European Union*. Luxembourg: Publications Office of the European Union.

Facht, Ulrika, ed. 2012. *Mediesverige 2012 mini*. Gøteborg: Nordicom.

Fagerjord, Anders, and Tanja Storsul. 2007. "Questioning Convergence." In *Ambivalence towards Convergence: Digitalization and Media Change*, edited by Tanja Storsul and Dagny Stuedal, 19–32. Göteborg: Nordicom.

Falkenberg, Vidar. 2010. "(R)evolution under Construction: The Dual History of Online Newspapers and Newspapers Online." In *Web History*, edited by Niels Brügger, 233–54. New York: Peter Lang.

Fenton, Natalie. 2011. "Deregulation or Democracy? New Media, News, Neoliberalism and the Public Interest." *Continuum* 25 (1): 63–72.

Ferro, Charles. 2008. "A Fragile Creature That Needs Care." In *Copyright Norden. The Nordic Model—Fact or Fiction?*, edited by Jesper Schou-Knudsen and the Nordic Council and Nordic Council of Ministers' Communications Department, 45–53. Copenhagen: Nordic Council and Nordic Council of Ministers.

FICORA. 2011. *Communication Markets in Finland 2010*. Helsinki: Finnish Communications Regulatory Authority.

Findahl, Olle. 2010a. *Swedes and the Internet 2010*. Stockholm: The Internet Infrastructure Foundation.

Findahl, Olle. 2010b. *Äldre svenskar och internet 2010*. Stockholm: The Internet Infrastructure Foundation.

Finnemann, Niels Ole, and Bo Hovgaard Thomasen. 2005. "Denmark. Multiplying News." In *Print and Online Newspapers in Europe. A Comparative Analysis in 16 Countries*, edited by Richard Van Der Wurff and Edmund Lauf, 91–104. Amsterdam: Het Spinhuis.

Flew, Terry. 2008. *New Media: An Introduction*. 3rd ed. South Melbourne: Oxford University Press.

Flisen, Terje. 2010. "Ramverk för public service-medierna i Norden." In *Nordiska public service-medier i den digitala mediekulturen: Pengar, politiken och publiken*, edited by Ulla Carlsson and Eva Harrie, 105–17. Gøteborg: Nordicom.

Freedman, Des. 2008. *The Politics of Media Policy*. Cambridge: Polity Press.

Freedom House. 2011. http://www.freedomhouse.org/template.cfm?page=251&year=2011. Accessed June 18, 2012.

From, Johan. 2009. *Fristilling og Fornyelse: Telenor fra verk til bedrift*. Oslo: Gyldendal Akademisk.

Froomkin, A. Michael. 2004. "Technologies for Democracy." In *Democracy Online: The Prospects for Political Renewal through the Internet*, edited by Peter M. Shane, 3–20. New York and London: Routledge.

Furre, Berge. 1991. *Vårt hundreår: Norsk historie 1905–1990*. Oslo: Det Norske Samlaget.

Futsæther, Knut-Arne, and Katja Møglestue. 2010. "Daglig dekning for nasjonale mediehus." *Forbruker & Media*. *TNS Gallup*. http://www.tns-gallup.no/arch/_img/9095037.ppt#1005,1. Accessed February 16, 2013.

Galperin, Hernan. 2004. *New Television, Old Politics: The Transition to Digital TV in the United States and Britain*. Cambridge: Cambridge University Press.

Garnham, Nicholas. 1986. "The Media and the Public Sphere." In *Communicating Poli-*

tics: Mass Communications and the Political Process, edited by Peter Golding, Graham Murdock, and Philip Schlesinger, 37–54. Leicester: Leicester University.

Garrard, Garry A. 1998. *Cellular Communications: Worldwide Market Development*. Norwood, MA: Artech House.

Gilder, George F. 1994. *Life after Television*. New York: W. W. Norton.

Gjesteland, Elisabeth. 2012. "Twitter som Nyhetskilde." In *Mediene & Terroraksjonen. Studier av Norske Mediers Dekning av 22. Juli*, edited by Svein Brurås, 129–54. Oslo: Unipub.

Goggin, Gerard. 2006. *Cell Phone Culture: Mobile Technology in Everyday Life*. London: Routledge.

Graham, Mark. 2011. "Time Machines and Virtual Portals. The Spatialities of the Digital Divide." *Progress in Development Studies* 11 (3): 211–27.

Grewal, David. 2010. "The Return of the State." *Harvard International Review*, February 1. http://hir.harvard.edu/big-ideas/the-return-of-the-state. Accessed November 20, 2013.

Gundersen, Hege. 2005. "Historisk og fiktivt. En studie av tv-seriene Heimat, Matador, og Vestavind." PhD diss. Oslo: University of Oslo.

Gunter, Barrie. 2003. *News and the Net*. Mahwah, NJ: Lawrence Erlbaum.

Gustafsson, Karl Erik, and Per Rydén. 2010. *A History of the Press in Sweden*. Göteborg: Nordicom.

Hadenius, Stig, Lennart Weibull, and Ingela Wadbring. 2011. *Massmedier: Press, radio och tv i den digitala tidsåldern*, 10th ed. Stockholm: Ekerlids.

Hagen, Anders W. 2012. "Vokser på å gi bort aviser." *Dagens Næringsliv*, March 2.

Hagen, Ingunn. 1992. "News Viewing Ideals and Everyday Practices: The Ambivalences of Watching Dagsrevyen." PhD diss., University of Bergen.

Hall, Peter A., and David Soskice. 2001. "An Introduction to Varieties of Capitalism." In *Varieties of Capitalism: The Institutional Foundations of Comparative Advantage*, edited by Peter A. Hall and David Soskice, 1–68. Oxford: Oxford University Press.

Hall, Stuart. 1992. "Which Public, Whose Service?" In *All Our Futures. The Changing Role and Purpose of the BBC*, edited by Wilf Stevenson, 23–38. London: British Film Institute.

Hallin, Daniel C., and Paolo Mancini. 2004. *Comparing Media Systems: Three Models of Media and Politics*. Cambridge: Cambridge University Press.

Hallin, Daniel C., and Paolo Mancini, eds. 2012a. *Comparing Media Systems beyond the Western World*. Cambridge, UK: Cambridge University Press.

Hallin, Daniel C., and Paolo Mancini. 2012b. "Comparing Media Systems: A Response to Critics." In *The Handbook of Comparative Communication Research*, edited by Frank Esser and Thomas Hanitzsch, 207–20. New York and London: Routledge.

Hansen, Erik Jørgen, Stein Ringen, Hannu Uusitalo, and Robert Eriksen, eds. 1993. *Welfare Trends in the Scandinavian Countries*. London and Armonk, NY: M. E. Sharpe.

Hardy, Jonathan. 2008. *Western Media Systems*. New York: Routledge.

Hardy, Jonathan. 2012. "Comparing Media Systems." In *The Handbook of Comparative Communication Research*, edited by Frank Esser and Thomas Hanitzsch, 185–206. New York and London: Routledge.

Harrie, Eva. 2010. "Radio och TV-landskapet i Norden." In *Nordiska public service-medier i den digitala mediekulturen: Pengar, politiken och publiken*, edited by Ulla Carlsson and Eva Harrie, 43–101. Göteborg: Nordicom.

Harvey, David. 2005. *A Brief History of Neoliberalism*. Oxford and New York: Oxford University Press.

Heinonen, Ari. 1998. "The Finnish Journalist: Watchdog with a Conscience." In *The Global Journalist: News People around the World*, edited by David H. Weaver, 161–213. Cresskill, NJ: Hampton Press.

Heinonen, Ari, and Terhi Kinnunen. 2005. "Finland. Cautious Online Strategies." In *Print and Online Newspapers in Europe. A Comparative Analysis in 16 Countries*, edited by Richard Van Der Wurff and Edmund Lauf, 117–30. Amsterdam: Het Spinhuis.

Hellman, Heikki. 1996. "The Formation of Television in Finland: A Case in Pragmatist Media Policy." In *Television in Scandinavia: History, Politics and Aesthetics*, edited by Ib Bondebjerg and Francesco Bono, 91–112. Luton: John Libbey Media.

Hellman, Heikki, and Toumo Sauri. 1994. "Public Service Television and the Tendency towards Convergence: Trends in Prime-Time Programme Structure in Finland, 1970–92." *Media, Culture & Society* 16 (1): 47–69.

Hendricks, John Allen, and Robert E. Denton, Jr., eds. 2010. *Communicator-in-Chief: How Barack Obama Used New Technology to Win the White House*. Lanham, MD: Lexington Books.

Herkman, Juha. 2009. "The Structural Transformation of the Democratic Corporatist Model: The Case of Finland." *Javnost* 16 (4): 73–90.

Hilson, Mary. 2008. *The Nordic Model: Scandinavia since 1945*. London: Reaktion Books.

Hjarvard, Stig. 1997. "Den globale virkelighed." In *Dansk mediehistorie: 1960–1995*, vol. 3, edited by Ib Bondebjerg and Klaus Bruhn Jensen, 44–53. Copenhagen: Samleren.

Hjarvard, Stig. 1999. *TV-nyheder i konkurrance*. Fredriksberg: Samfundslitteratur.

Hjeltnes, Guri, ed. 2010. *Norsk presses historie 1660–2010. Imperiet vakler 1945–2010*. Oslo: Universitetsforlaget.

Hoffmann-Riem, Wolfgang. 1996. *Regulating Media. The Licensing and Supervision of Broadcasting in Six Countries*. New York: The Guilford Press.

Höijer, Birgitta. 1998. *Det hørde vi allihop! Etermedierna och publiken under 1990-tallet*. Stockholm: Stiftelsen Etermedierna i Sverige.

Hollifield, C. Ann. 2004. "The Economics of International Media." In *Media Economics: Theory and Practice*, 3rd ed., edited by Alison Alexander, James Owers, Rod Caveth, C. Ann Hollifield, and Albert N. Greco, 85–106. London and Mahwah, NJ: Lawrence Erlbaum.

Høst, Sigurd. 2011. *Avisåret 2010*, Rapport nr. 18/2011. Høgskulen i Volda og Møreforsking Volda.

Høst, Sigurd. 2012. *Avisåret 2011*. Rapport nr. 29/2012. Høgskulen i Volda og Møreforsking Volda.

Høyer, Svennik. 2005. "The Rise and Fall of the Scandinavian Party Press." In *Diffusion of the News Paradigm 1850–2000*, edited by Svennik Høyer and Horst Pöttker, 75–92. Göteborg: Nordicom.

Høyer, Svennik, Stig Hadenius, and Lennart Weibull. 1975. *The Politics and Economics of the Press: A Developmental Perspective*. London: Sage.

Hujanen, Taisto. 2004. "Content Production at the New Identity of Public Service Broadcasting: The Case of Digital Television." Paper presented at RIPE@2004, Aarhus, Denmark, June 3–5.

Humphreys, Peter J. 1996. *Mass Media and Media Policy in Western Europe*. Manchester: Manchester University Press.

Humphreys, Peter J. 2012. "A Political Scientist's Contribution to the Comparative Study of Media Systems in Europe: A Response to Hallin and Mancini." In *Trends in Communication Policy Research: New Theories, Methods & Subjects*, edited by Natascha Just and Manuel Puppis, 157–76. Bristol: Intellect.

Hyde, Adam, Mike Linksvayer, kanarinka, Michael Mandiberg, Marta Peirano, Sissu Tarka, Astra Taylor, Alan Toner, and Mushon Zer-Aviv. 2012. "What Is Collaboration Anyway?" In *The Social Media Reader*, edited by Michael Mandiberg, 53–70. New York: New York University Press.

ICA. 2013. *Global Communications and National Policies: The Return of the State?* International Communication Association (ICA) Preconference. June 16. London: University of Westminster.

IFPI. 2010. "Digital Music Report 2010. Music How, When, Where You Want It." http://www.ifpi.org/content/library/dmr2010.pdf. Accessed January 23, 2012.

IFPI. 2011. "Digital Music Report 2011. Music at the Touch of a Button." http://www.ifpi.org/content/library/DMR2011.pdf. Accessed January 23, 2012.

Ihlebæk, Karoline A., Trine Syvertsen, and Espen Ytreberg. 2011. "Farvel til mangfoldet?—Endringer i norske TV-kanalers programlegging og sendeskjemaer etter digitaliseringen." *Norsk Medietidsskrift* 18 (3): 217–36.

Interbrand. 2009. "The Best Global Brands 2009." http://www.interbrand.com/en/best-global-brands/previous-years/best-global-brands-2009.aspx. Accessed October 31, 2013.

Interbrand. 2013. "The Best Global Brands 2013." http://www.interbrand.com/en/best-global-brands/2013/Nokia. Accessed October 31, 2013.

International Telecommunication Union. 2011. "Measuring the Information Society." Geneve: ITU. http://ictlogy.net/bibliography/reports/projects.php?idp=2042. Accessed June 14, 2012.

International Telecommunication Union. 2012. "Measuring the Information Society." Geneve: ITU. http://www.itu.int/ITU-D/ict/publications/idi/index.html. Accessed February 15, 2013.

Iosifidis, P. 2011. *Global Media and Communication Policy*. London: Palgrave MacMillan.

Jakubowicz, Karol. 2008. "Hold fast i kernen, og lav så om på (nesten) alt det andet! Redefininering av public service broadcasting for det 21. Århundrede." In *Public Service i netværkssamfundet*, edited and translated by Frands Mortensen, 251–82. Forlaget Samfundslitteratur: Fredriksberg. Originally published as "Keep the Essence, Change (Almost) Everything Else. Redefining PSB for the 21st Century," in *Public Service Broadcasting in the Age of Globalization*, edited by Indrajit Banerjee and Kalinga Seneviratne (Singapore: Asian Media Information and Communication Centre, 2006).

Jenkins, Henry. 2006. *Convergence Culture: Where Old and New Media Collide*. New York: New York University Press.

Jensen, Klaus Bruhn, ed. 1997. *Dansk Mediehistorie 1960–1995*. Vol. 3. Copenhagen: Samleren.

Jensen, Klaus Bruhn, ed. 2003. *Dansk Mediehistorie 1995–2003*. Vol. 4. Fredriksberg: Samfundslitteratur.

Jensen, Pia Majbritt. 2007. "Television Format Adaptation in a Trans-national Perspective. An Australian and Danish Case Study." PhD diss., University of Aarhus.

Jessop, Bob. 2010. "The 'Return' of the National State in the Current Crisis of the World Market." *Capital & Class*. 34 (1): 38–43.

Kackman, Michael, Marnie Binfield, Matthew Thomas Payne, Allison Perlman, and Bryan Sebok, eds. 2011. *Flow TV: Television in the Age of Media Convergence*. New York: Routledge.

Kampanje. 2010. "Dansk avis raser mot Apple-sensur av nakne damer." October 12. http://www.kampanje.com/medier/article5343257.ece. Accessed February 16, 2013.

Karlsen, Faltin, Vilde Schanke Sundet, Trine Syvertsen, and Espen Ytreberg. 2009. "Non-Professional Activity on Television in a Time of Digitalisation. More Fun for the Elite or New Opportunities for Ordinary People?" *Nordicom Review* 30 (1): 19–36.

Karlson, Michael. 2006. "Nätjournalistik—En explorativ fallstudie av digitala mediers karaktärsdrag på fyra nyhetssajter." PhD diss., Lunds Universitet.

Karlsson, Magnus. 1998. "The Liberalisation of Telecommunications in Sweden: Technology and Regime Change from the 1960s to 1993." PhD diss., Linköping University.

Karppinen, Kari, Hannu Nieminen, and Anna-Laura Markkanen. 2011. "Finland: High Professional Ethos in a Small, Concentrated Media Market." In *The Media for Democracy Monitor. A Cross National Study of Leading News Media*, edited by Josef Trappel, Hannu Nieminen, and Lars Nord, 113–42. Göteborg: Nordicom.

Kildal, Nanna, and Stein Kuhnle, eds. 2005. *Normative Foundations of the Welfare State: The Nordic Experience*. London and New York: Routledge.

King, Anthony. 1998. "Thatcherism and the Emergence of Sky Television." *Media, Culture & Society* 20 (2): 277–93.

Kjær, Peter, and Tore Slaatta, eds. 2007. *Mediating Business: The Expansion of Business Journalism*. Frederiksberg, Copenhagen, DNK: Copenhagen Business School Press.

Kjølsrød, Lise. 2003. "En tjenesteintens velferdsstat." In *Det Norske samfunn*, 4th ed., edited by Ivar Frønes and Lise Kjølsrød, 184–209. Oslo: Gyldendal Akademisk.

Kleberg, Madeleine. 1996. "The History of Swedish Television—Three Stages." In *Television in Scandinavia, History, Politics and Aesthetics*, edited by Ib Bondebjerg and Francesco Bono, 182–207. Luton: John Libbey Media.

Knudsen, Erik. 2013. "Media Coverage as Attitude Source: A Study of Second-Level Agenda Setting at the Outbreak of a Norwegian Welfare Crisis." Paper presented at Nordmedia Conference, August 8–11. Oslo.

Korpi, Walter. 1978. *The Working Class in Welfare Capitalism: Work, Unions and Politics in Sweden*. London: Routledge & Kegan Paul.

Krebber, Daniel. 2002. *Europeanisation of Regulatory Television Policy. The Decision-making Process of the Television without Frontiers Directives from 1989 & 1997*. Baden-Baden: Nomos.

Kuhnle, Stein, ed. 2000. *Survival of the European Welfare State*. London and New York: Routledge.

Le Foulon, Marie-Laure. 2008. "Homo Nordicus, A Paradoxical Figure." In *Copyright Norden. The Nordic Model—Fact or Fiction?*, edited by Jesper Schou-Knudsen and the Nordic Council and Nordic Council of Ministers' Communications Department, 19–30. Copenhagen: Nordic Council and Nordic Council of Ministers.

Lessig, Lawrence. 2008. *Remix: Making Art and Commerce Thrive in the Hybrid Economy*. New York: Penguin.

Levy, David A. L. 1999. *Europe's Digital Revolution. Broadcasting Regulation, the EU and the Nation State*. London and New York: Routledge.

Lindholm, Tomi. 2010. "Analysing and Comparing the Histories of Web Strategies of Major Media Companies—Case Finland." In *Web History*, edited by Niels Brügger, 195–212. New York: Peter Lang.

Lindt, Knut. 1984. *Østenfor VG og Vestenfor Blindern*. Oslo: Dreyer.

Lotz, Amanda D. 2007. *The Television Will Be Revolutionized*. New York: New York University Press.

Ludes, Peter, ed. 2008. *Convergence and Fragmentation: Media Technology and the Information Society*. Bristol, UK and Chicago: Intellect.

Lund, Anker B., Karin Raeymaeckers, and Josef Trappel. 2011. "Newspapers: Adapting and Experimenting." In *Media in Europe Today*, edited by Josef Trappel, Werner A. Meier, Leen d'Haenens, Jeanette Steemers, and Barbara Thomass, 43–59. Bristol: Intellect.

Löfgren, Orvar. 1990. "Medierna i nationsbygget. Hur press, radio och TV gjort Sverige svenskt." In *Medier och kulturer*, edited by Ulf Hannerz, 85–121. Stockholm: Carlssons.

Løvheim, Mia. 2011. "Personal and Popular: The Case of Young Swedish Female Top-bloggers." *Nordicom Review* 32 (1): 3–16.

Maasø, Arnt, Vilde Schanke Sundet, and Trine Syvertsen. 2007. "'Fordi de fortjener det.' Publikumsdeltakelse som strategisk utviklingsområde I mediebransjen." *Norsk Medietidsskrift* 14 (2): 125–53.

Maasø, Arnt, and Ragnhild Toldnes. 2014. "Mitt lille land: Sørgemusikk og sosiale strømmer." In *Musikk og 22. juli*, edited by Jan Sverre Knudsen, Marie S. Skånland, and Gro Trondalen. Oslo: Norges musikkhøgskole.

Maier-Rabler, Ursula. 2008. "ePolicies in Europe: A Human-Centric and Culturally Biased Approach." In *Convergence and Fragmentation: Media Technology and the Information Society*, edited by Peter Ludes, 47–66. Bristol and Chicago: Intellect.

Mandiberg, Michael, ed. 2012. *The Social Media Reader*. New York: New York University Press.

Mayfield, Ross. 2006. "Power Law of Participation." *Ross Mayfield's Weblog*, April 27. http://ross.typepad.com/blog/2006/04/power_law_of_pa.html. Accessed August 2, 2013.

McKinsey & Company. 2004. "Review of Public Service Broadcasting around the World." http://www.ofcom.org.uk/consult/condocs/psb2/psb2/psbwp/wp3mck.pdf. Accessed April 10, 2007.

McQuail, Denis, and Karen Siune, eds. 1986. *New Media Politics: Comparative Perspectives in Western Europe*. London: Sage.

McQuail, Denis, and Karen Siune, eds. 1998. *Media Policy: Convergence, Concentration and Commerce*. London: Sage.

MedieNorge. 2010. "Opplagstall norske aviser." http://medienorge.uib.no/?cat=statistikk&page=avis&queryID=190. Accessed January 23, 2012.

MedieNorge. 2013a. "Daglig dekning for mediehus og konsern. Schibsted 2012." http://www.medienorge.uib.no/?cat=statistikk&medium=avis&queryID=366. Accessed November 1, 2013.

MedieNorge. 2013b. "Avis—TNS Gallup—Forbruker & Media." http://medienorge.uib.no/?cat=statistikk&page=avis. Accessed November 28, 2013.

Meikle, Graham, and Sherman Young. 2012. *Media Convergence. Networked Digital Media in Everyday Life*. Basingstoke: Palgrave Macmillan.

Mendel, Toby. 2000. "Public Service Broadcasting. A Comparative Legal Survey." Kuala

Lumpur: UNESCO, Asia Pacific Institute for Broadcasting Development. http://www.unesco.org/webworld/publications/mendel/jaya_index.html. Accessed January 23, 2012.

Microsoft. 2013. "Microsoft to Acquire Nokia's Devices & Services Business, License Nokia's Patents and Mapping Services." http://www.microsoft.com/en-us/news/press/2013/sep13/09-02announcementpr.aspx. Accessed October 17, 2013.

Mjøs, Ole J. 2010a. *Media Globalization and the Discovery Channel Networks*. London and New York: Routledge.

Mjøs, Ole. J. 2010b. "The Symbiosis of Children's Television and Merchandising: Comparative Perspectives of the Norwegian Public Service Broadcaster, NRK, and the Global Disney Channel." *Media, Culture & Society* 32 (6): 1031–42.

Mjøs, Ole. J. 2011 "A Marriage of Convenience? European Public Broadcasters' Cross-National Partnerships in Factual Television." *International Communications Gazette* 73 (3): 181–97.

Mjøs, Ole J. 2012. *Music, Social Media and Global Mobility*. London and New York: Routledge.

Mjøset, Lars. 2011. "Nordic Political Economy after Financial Deregulation: Banking Crises, Economic Experts, and the Role of Neoliberalism." In *The Nordic Varieties of Capitalism*, edited by Lars Mjøset, 365–420. Bingley: Emerald Group Publishing Limited.

Moe, Hallvard. 2003. "Digitaliseringen av fjernsyn og allmennkringkastingens skjebne." Master's thesis. Published as report no 54, University of Bergen.

Moe, Hallvard. 2009. *Public Broadcasters, the Internet, and Democracy. Comparing Policy and Exploring Public Service Media Online*. Bergen: University of Bergen.

Moe, Hallvard. 2010. "Governing Public Service Broadcasting: 'Public Value Tests' in Different National Contexts." *Communication, Culture & Critique* 3 (2): 207–23.

Moe, Hallvard. 2012a. "Between Public Service and Commercial Venture: The Norwegian Broadcasting Corporation on the Web 1994–2000." In *Histories of Public Service Broadcasters on the Web*, edited by Maureen Burns and Niels Brügger, 75–90. New York: Peter Lang.

Moe, Hallvard. 2012b. "How to Preserve the Broadcasting License Fee: The Case of Norway." *Journal of Media Business Studies* 9 (1): 55–69.

Moe, Hallvard. 2012c. "Det underforståtte i mediepolitikken. Eksempelet formidlingsplikt." *Nordicom Information* 34 (1): 23–37.

Moe, Hallvard. 2013. "Public Service Broadcasting and Social Networking Sites: The Norwegian Broadcasting Corporation on Facebook." *Media International Australia* 146:114–22.

Moe, Hallvard, and Anders O. Larsson. 2012a. "Studying Political Microblogging. Twitter Users in 2010 Swedish Election Campaign." *New Media & Society* 14 (5): 729–47.

Moe, Hallvard, and Anders O. Larsson. 2012b. "Twitterbruk under valgkampen 2011" (Twitter use during the Norwegian 2011 election). *Norsk Medietidsskrift*, 19 (2): 151–62.

Moe, Hallvard, and Ole J. Mjøs. 2013. "The Arm's Length Principle in Nordic Public Broadcasting Regulation." In *Public Service Media from a Nordic Horizon. Politics, Markets, Programming and Users*, edited by Ulla Carlsson, 75–92. Göteborg, Nordicom.

Moe, Hallvard, and Helle Sjøvaag. 2009. "The Challenges of Comparing Media Systems—An Interview with Daniel C. Hallin." *Journal of Global Mass Communication* 1 (3–4): 132–41.

Moe, Hallvard, and Trine Syvertsen. 2009. "Researching Public Service Broadcasting." In *The Handbook of Journalism Studies*, edited by Karin Wahl-Jorgensen and Thomas Hanitzsch, 398–412. New York and London: Routledge.

Moen, Eli, and Kari Lilja. 2005. "Change in Coordinated Market Economies: The Case of Nokia and Finland." In *Changing Capitalisms? Internationalization, Institutional Change, and Systems of Economic Organization*, edited by Glenn Morgan, Richard Whitley, and Eli Moen, 352–79. Oxford: Oxford University Press.

Mortensen, Frands. 2005. "Er licensen til public service-institutionerne i Norden lovlig statsstøtte ifølge EU?" *Nordisk Kulturpolitisk Tidskrift* 8 (1): 84–119.

MTG. 2012. Annual Report.

MTG. 2013. Interim report, Q3. http://www.mtg.se/en/investors/quarterly-reports/q3-2013-interim-report-january-september/. Accessed November 20, 2013.

Murdock, Graham, and Peter Golding. 1977. "Capitalism, Communication and Class Relations." In *Mass Communication and Society*, edited by James Curran, Michael Gurevitch, and Janet Woollacott, 12–43. London: Arnold/Open University Press.

Negroponte, Nicholas. 1995. *Being Digital*, 1st ed. New York: Knopf.

Nieminen, Hannu. 2013. "Challenges of Convergence to Media and Communications Regulation: Tools for Analysis." Paper presented at NordMedia Conference, August 8–11, Oslo

Nokia. 2011. "Nokia Outlines New Strategy, Introduces New Leadership." February 11. http://press.nokia.com/2011/02/11/nokia-outlines-new-strategy-introduces-new-leadership-operational-structure/. Accessed March 14, 2013.

Nokia. 2013a. "The Nokia Story." http://www.nokia.com/global/about-nokia/about-us/the-nokia-story/. Accessed November 20, 2013.

Nokia. 2013b. "Nokia to Sell Devices & Services Business to Microsoft in EUR 5,44 billion in All-Cash Transaction." http://press.nokia.com/2013/09/03/nokia-to-sell-devices-services-business-to-microsoft-in-eur-5-44-billion-all-cash-transaction/. Accessed November 20, 2013.

Nokia Group. 2003. Annual Report.

Nokia Group. 2004. Annual Report.

Nokia Group. 2005. Annual Report.

Nokia Group. 2006. Annual Report.

Nokia Group. 2007. Annual Report.

Nokia Group. 2008. Annual Report.

Nokia Group. 2009. Annual Report.

Nokia Group. 2010. Annual Report.

Nokia Group. 2011. Annual Report.

Nokia Group. 2012. Annual Report.

Nord, Lars. 2008. "Comparing Nordic Media Systems: North between West and East?" *Central European Journal of Communication* 1 (1): 95–110.

Nord, Lars, and Marie Grusell. 2012. *Inte för smalt, inte för brett. Spelet om framtidens public service*. Göteborg: Nordicom.

Norden. 2012. "'Nordic Model' Patent Dispute Attracts International Attention." http://www.norden.org/en/news-and-events/news/nordic-model-patent-dispute-attracts-international-attention. Accessed September 24.

Nordenstreng, Kaarle. 2006. "'Four Theories of the Press' Reconsidered." In *Researching Media, Democracy and Participation*, edited by Nico Carpentier, Pille Pruulmann-Vengerfeldt, Kaarle Nordenstreng, Maren Hartmann, Peeter Vihalemm, and Bart Cammaerts, 35–45. Tartu: Tartu University Press.

Nordic Council. 2012. "'Nordic Model' Patent Dispute Attracts International Attention." March 14. http://www.norden.org/en/news-and-events/nordic-model-patent-dispute-attracts-international-attention. Accessed January 16.

Nordicom. 2006. *Media Trends 2006: Radio, TV & Internet.* Göteborg: Nordicom.

Nordicom. 2009. *The Nordic Media Market: Denmark Finland Iceland Norway Sweden, Media Companies and Business Activities.* 2nd ed. Compiled by Eva Harrie. Göteborg: Nordicom.

Nordicom. 2010a. *A Sampler of International Media and Communication Statistics 2010.* Edited by Sara Leckner and Ulrika Facht. Göteborg: Nordicom.

Nordicom. 2010b. "Top Ten Web Sites, Ranked by Number of Unique Visitors per Week 2010, Week 34 or 41, August, October." http://www.nordicom.gu.se/common/stat_xls/1882_9550_websites2010.xls. Accessed January 23, 2012.

Nordicom. 2012a. "Purpose of Individuals' Use of Internet 2003–2010." http://www.nordicom.gu.se/eng.php?portal=mt&main=showStatTranslate.php&me=1&media=PC%20and%20Internet&type=media&translation=PC%20och%20internet. Accessed April 12, 2012.

Nordicom. 2012b. "The Largest Newspaper Companies in Finland, Norway and Sweden 2012 by Share of Circulation." http://www.nordicom.gu.se/eng.php?portal=mt&main=showStatTranslate.php&me=1&media=Newspapers&type=media&translation=Dagspress. Accessed November 29, 2013.

Nordicom. 2012c. "Access to Internet at Home 2001–2011." http://www.nordicom.gu.se/eng.php?portal=mt&main=showStatTranslate.php&me=1&mmedi=PC%20and%20Internet&type=media&translation=PC%20och%20internet. Accessed November 26, 2013.

Nordicom. 2012d. *Public Service Media in the Nordic Countries*, compiled by Eva Harrie, Göteborg: Nordicom.

Nordvision. 2012. "Årsrapport 2011." http://www.nordvision.org/fileadmin/webmasterfiles/AArsrapporter/NV2011_2012_screen_view.pdf. Accessed March 7, 2013.

Norland, Andreas. 2001. *Bly blir gull. Schibsteds historie 1839–1933*, 1. Oslo: Schibsted forlag.

Norland, Andreas. 2011. *Medier, makt og millioner. Schibsteds historie 1934–2011*, 2. Oslo: Schibsted forlag

NOU. 1972. "Norsk Rikskringkasting—Organisasjon og ansettelsesvilkår." Kringkastingslovutvalget, Dæhlin Rapport I. 1972: 25.

NOU. 1992. "Mål og midler i pressepolitikken." *Dagspresseutvalget.* 1992: 14. Oslo: Kulturdepartementet.

NOU. 2000. "Pressepolitikk ved et tusenårsskifte." *Dagspresseutvalgets instilling.* 2000: 15. Oslo: Statens Forvaltningstjeneste, Informasjonsforvaltning.

NOU. 2010. "Lett å komme til orde, vanskelig å bli hørt—en moderne mediestøtte." Mediestøtteutvalgets utredning. 2010: 14. Oslo: Departementenes Servicesenter, Informasjonsforvaltning.

NRK. 2001. "1,7 millioner så vielsen." http://www.nrk.no/nyheter/innenriks/kongehuset/kronprinsbryllupet/sendinger/1242958.html. Accessed November 28, 2013.

NRK. 2011. *NRKs Profilundersøkelse.* http://nrk.no/informasjon/nyheter_om_nrk/1.8044316. Accessed November 2013.

NRK. 2012. "NRK i tall." http://www.nrk.no/aarsrapport/2011/statistikk. Accessed March 13, 2013.

Nygren, Gunnar, and Maria Zuiderveld, eds. 2011. *En himla många kanaler. Flerkanalpublicering I svenska mediehus.* Göteborg: Nordicom.

O'Reilly, Tim. 2012. "What Is Web 2.0?" In *The Social Media Reader*, edited by Michael Mandiberg, 32–52. New York: New York University Press.

Østbye, Helge. 1982. "Norsk Rikskringkasting: Ett monopol—to medier." In *Maktutredningen: Rapporten om massemedier*, NOU: 30, 241–99. Oslo: Universitetsforlaget.

Østbye, Helge. 1995. *Mediepolitikk. Skal medieutviklingen styres?* Oslo: Universitetsforlaget.

Ottosen, Rune, Lars Arve Røssland, and Helge Østbye. 2002. *Norsk Pressehistorie*. Oslo: Det Norske Samlaget.

Ottosen, Rune, and Arne H. Krumsvik. 2008. "Digitale medier og redaksjonell endring—noen sentrale utviklingstrekk." In *Journalistikk i en digital hverdag*, edited by Rune Ottosen and Arne H. Krumsvik, 12–39. Kristiansand: IJ-forlaget.

Ozanich, Gary W., and Michael O. Wirth. 2004. "Structure and Change: A Communications Industry Overview." In *Media Economics: Theory and Practice*, 3rd ed., edited by Alison Alexander, James Owers, Rod Carveth, C. Ann Hollifield, and Albert N. Greco, 69–84. London and Mahwah, NJ: Lawrence Erlbaum.

Parmann, Marius. 2010. "Norge uten daglige gratisaviser: en stabil situasjon?" Master's thesis, University of Oslo.

Paulsen, Gard Erland. 2010. "Noe for alle. Alltid? NRK sett gjennom flerkulturelle briller." Master's thesis, University of Oslo.

Pedersen, Ove K. 2011. Konkurrencestaten. København: Hans Reitzels Forlag.

Peters, Thomas J. 1992. *Liberation Management: Necessary Disorganization for the Nanosecond Nineties*. New York: Knopf.

Picard, Robert G. 1988. *The Ravens of Odin: The Press in the Nordic Nations*. Ames: Iowa State University Press.

Post-og teletilsynet. 2009. *Telecommunication Markets in the Nordic Countries*. Lillesand: Post-og teletilsynet.

Post-og teletilsynet. 2010. *Høykapasitetsnett—Utbygging og økt valgfrihet for brukerne. Mulige tiltak, forretningsmodeller og framtidig regulering*. Lillesand: Post-og teletilsynet.

Pulkkinen, Matti. 1997. *The Breakthrough of Nokia Mobile Phones*. Helsinki: HSE Series A-122.

Quandt, Thorsten. 2008. "(No) News on the World Wide Web? A Comparative Content Analysis of Online News in Europe and the United States." *Journalism Studies* 9 (5): 717–38.

Raaum, Odd. 2001. "Pressefrihetens røtter og første nyttevekster." In *Fra Eidsvoll til Marienlyst. Studier i norske mediers historie fra Grunnloven til TV-alderen*, edited by Henrik G. Bastiansen and Øystein Meland, 10–34. Kristiansand: Høyskoleforlaget.

Raboy, Marc, ed. 1996. *Public Broadcasting for the 21st Century*. Academia Research Monograph 17. Luton: University of Luton Press.

Rasmussen, Jacob. 2003. "Den gode, den onde og den virkelig sjove indvandrer" (The good, the bad and the really funny immigrant). *Jordens folk—etnografisk tidsskrift* 38 (2): 8–13.

Rasmussen, Terje. 2006. *Nettmedier. Journalistikk og medier på Internett*. 2nd ed. Bergen: Fagbokforlaget.

Refslund Christensen, Dorthe, and Kjetil Sandvik. 2013. "Sharing Death: Conceptions of Time at a Danish Online Memorial Site." In *Taming Time, Timing Death: Social Technologies and Ritual*, edited by Dorthe Refslund Christensen and Rane Willerslev, 99–118. Farnham: Ashgate.

Reith, John. 1924. *Broadcast over Britain*. London: Hodder and Stoughton.

Reporters Without Borders. 2010. "Press Freedom Index 2010." http://en.rsf.org/press-freedom-index-2010,1034.html. Accessed February 25, 2013.

Reporters Without Borders. 2012. "Press Freedom Index 2011/2012." http://en.rsf.org/press-freedom-index-2011–2012,1043.html. Accessed February 25, 2013.

Reporters Without Borders. 2013. "Press Freedom Index 2013." http://en.rsf.org/press-freedom-index-2013,1054.html.

Rettberg, Jill W. 2008. *Blogging*. Cambridge: Polity Press.

Rheingold, Howard. 1994. *The Virtual Community: Homesteading on the Electronic Frontier*. New York: Harper Perennial.

Rosen, Christine. 2004. "The Age of Egocasting." *The New Atlantis Fall 2004–Winter 2005*. http://www.thenewatlantis.com/publications/the-age-of-egocasting. Accessed October 6, 2012.

Ryssdal, Rolv Erik. 2011a. *Mediefusjon for fremtiden*. Dagens Næringsliv. March 10.

Ryssdal, Rolv Erik. 2011b. *Schibsted og medieierskapsloven*, November 9. Høringsdokument til Medieeierskapsutredningen. http://www.schibsted.no/Pressesenter/Nyheter/2011/Schibsted-og-Medieeierskapsloven. Accessed November 20, 2013.

Salokangas, Raimo. 1999. "From Political to National, Regional, and Local: The Newspaper Structure in Finland." *Nordicom Review* 20 (1): 95–100.

Scannell, Paddy. 1989. "Public Service Broadcasting and Modern Public Life." *Media, Culture & Society* 11 (2): 135–66.

Scannell, Paddy. 1990. "Public Service Broadcasting: The History of a Concept." In *Understanding Television*, edited by Andrew Goodwin and Garry Whannel, 11–29. London: Routledge.

Scannell, Paddy, and David Cardiff. 1991. *A Social History of British Broadcasting*. Vol. 1, *1922–1939. Serving the Nation*. Oxford: Basil Blackwell.

Schibsted. 1995. Annual Report.

Schibsted. 2003. Annual Report.

Schibsted. 2005. Annual Report.

Schibsted. 2007. Annual Report.

Schibsted. 2008. Annual Report.

Schibsted. 2010. Annual Report.

Schibsted. 2012. Annual Report.

Schibsted. 2013a. "About Schibsted." http://www.schibsted.com/About-Schibsted/Schibsted-Sweden/. Accessed November 9, 2013.

Schibsted 2013b. "Om Schibsted." http://www.schibsted.no/Om-Schibsted/Historie. Accessed November 22, 2013.

Schibsted. 2013c. "Vårt samfunnsoppdrag." http://www.schibsted.no/Om-Schibsted/Vart- samfunnsoppdrag/Redaksjonell-frihet/#sthash.x97kZdx7.dpuf. Accessed November 20, 2013.

Schradie, Jen. 2011. "The Digital Production Gap: The Digital Divide and Web 2.0 Collide." *Poetics* 39 (2): 145–68.

Schultz, Ida. 2007. "Fra partipresse over Omnibuspresse til Segmentpresse—En sociologisk hypotese om dagspressens historiske udvikling" (From party press to omnibus press to a segmented press—a sociological hypothesis on the historical development of the Danish press system). *Journalistica* 5:5–26.

Siebert, Fred S., Theodore Peterson, and Wilbur Schramm. 1956. *Four Theories of the Press: The Authoritarian, Libertarian, Social Responsibility, and Soviet Communist Concepts of What the Press Should Be and Do*. Urbana: University of Illinois Press.

Siles, Ignacio, and Pablo J. Boczkowski. 2012. "Making Sense of the Newspaper Crises: A Critical Assessment of Existing Research and an Agenda for Future Work." *New Media & Society* 14 (8): 1375–94.

Simonnes, Kamilla. 2013. "Hissig nettdebatt gir mer fordommer." http://www.forskning.no/artikler/2013/september/366734. Accessed November 26, 2013.

Skirbekk, Gunnar. 1984. "Folkeopplysning—medium for folket." *Syn og Segn* 4:305–8.

Skogerbø, Eli, and Tanja Storsul. 2003. *Telesektoren i endring: mål, midler og marked*. Oslo: Unipub.

Skogerbø, Eli, and Trine Syvertsen. 2004. "Towards an Information Society? The Value of Media Production and Consumption." *Javnost—The Public* 11 (1): 45–60.

Skogerbø, Eli, and Trine Syvertsen. 2008. "Medieøkonomi og informasjonssamfunnet." In *Medievitenskap. Medier—institusjoner og historie*, 2nd ed., edited by Martin Eide, 113–34. Oslo: Fagbokforlaget.

Slagstad, Rune. 1998. *De nasjonale strateger*. Oslo: Pax.

Smith, Anthony. 1998. "Television as a Public Service Medium." In *Television: An International History*, edited by Anthony Smith and Richard Paterson, 38–54. New York: Oxford University Press.

Social Bakers. 2012. "Facebook Statistics by Country." http://www.socialbakers.com/facebook-statistics/. Accessed November 12, 2012.

Søndergaard, Henrik. 1994. *DR i TV-konkurrencens tidsalder*. Fredriksberg: Samfundslitteratur.

Søndergaard, Henrik. 1996. "Fundamentals in the History of Danish Television." In *Television in Scandinavia: History, Politics and Aesthetics*, edited by Ib Bondebjerg and Francesco Bono, 11–40. Luton: University of Luton Press.

Søndergaard, Henrik. 2008. "DR's digitale strategier." In *Public service i netværkssamfundet*, edited by Frands Mortensen, 31–66. Samfundslitteratur: Fredriksberg.

SOU. 1975. *Pressens funktioner I samhället - En forskningsrapport till 1972 års pressutredning*. Stockholm: Liber Förlag.

St. meld. nr. 14. 2007–2008. 2008. "Dataspill." http://www.regjeringen.no/nb/dep/kud/dok/regpubl/stmeld/2007–2008/stmeld-nr-14–2007–2008-.html?id=502808. Accessed January 23, 2012.

Steinbock, Dan. 2003. "Globalization of Wireless Value System: From Geographic to Strategic Advantages." *Telecommunication Policy* 27:207–35.

Steinbock, Dan. 2004. *What Next? Finnish ICT Cluster and Globalization*. 38. Helsinki: Sisäasiainministeriön Julkaisuja.

Steinbock, Dan. 2005. "Design and Mobile Innovation." *Design Management Review*. Fall.

Steinbock, Dan. 2010. *Winning across Global Markets: How Nokia Creates Strategic Advantage in a Fast-Changing World*. San Francisco: Jossey-Bass.

Stjernfelt, Frederik. 2009. "Pressure on Press Freedom: The Current Religious War on Freedom of Expression." In *Freedom of Speech Abridged? Cultural, Legal and Philosophical Challenges*, edited by Anine Kierulf and Helge Rønning, 129–37. Göteborg: Nordicom.

Storsul, Tanja. 2008. "Telecom Liberalization: Distributive Challenges and National Differences." In *Convergence and Fragmentation: Media Technology and the Information Society*, edited by Peter Ludes, 197–216. Bristol, UK, and Chicago: Intellect.

Storsul, Tanja, and Dagny Stuedahl, eds. 2007. *Ambivalence towards Convergence: Digitalization and Media Change*. Göteborg: Nordicom.

Storsul, Tanja, and Vilde Schanke Sundet. 2006. "Digital Terrestrial Television in Scandinavia." In *Digitising TV: Theoretical Issues and Comparative Studies across Europe*, edited by Fausto Colombo and Nicoletta Vittadini, 239–65. Milan: Vita e Pensiero.

Storsul, Tanja, and Trine Syvertsen. 2007. "The Impact of Convergence on European Television Policy: Pressure for Change—Forces of Stability." *Convergence* 13 (3): 275–98.

Strix. 2013. http://www.strix.se. Accessed November 20, 2013.

Strömbäck, Jesper, Mark Ørsten, and Toril Aalberg, eds. 2008. *Communicating Politics. Political Communication in the Nordic Countries*. Göteborg: Nordicom.

Sundet, Vilde Schanke. 2012. "Making Sense of Mobile Media. Institutional Working Notions, Strategies and Actions in Convergent Media Markets." PhD diss., Universiy of Oslo.

Sundin, Staffan. 2013. *Den svenska mediamarknaden*. Göteborg: Nordicom.

Sunstein, Cass R. 2001. *Republic.com*. Princeton, NJ: Princeton University Press.

SVT. 2012."Sveriges Televisions public service-redovisning 2011." http://www.svt.se/omsvt/fakta/public-service. Accessed August 1, 2013.

Syvertsen, Trine. 1991. "Public Television in Crisis: Critiques Compared in Norway and Britain." *European Journal of Communication* 6 (1): 95–114.

Syvertsen, Trine. 1992. "Public Television in Transition: A Comparative and Historical Analysis of the BBC and the NRK." PhD diss., University of Leicester.

Syvertsen, Trine. 1997. *Den store TV-krigen: Norsk allmennfjernsyn 1988–96*. Oslo: Fagbokforlaget.

Syvertsen, Trine. 1999. "The Many Uses of the 'Public Service' Concept." *Nordicom Review* 20 (1): 5–12.

Syvertsen, Trine. 2004. *Mediemangfold: Styring av mediene i et globalisert marked*. Kristiansand: IJ-Forlaget.

Syvertsen, Trine. 2006. "'-Vi har sett frem til denne dagen med forventning.' TV 2 som allmennkringkaster og mediebedrift." In *Et hjem for oss—Et hjem for deg? Analyser av TV 2*, 2nd ed., edited by Gunn Enli, Trine Syvertsen, and Susanne Ø. Sæther, 42–66. Kristiansand: IJ-forlaget.

Syvertsen, Trine. 2008. "Allmennkringkasting i krise—not!" *Norsk medietidsskrift* 15 (3): 211–36.

Syvertsen, Trine, and Eli Skogerbø. 1998. "Scandinavia, Netherlands, and Belgium." In *Television: An International History*, edited by Anthony Smith and Richard Paterson, 223–33. New York: Oxford University Press.

Thielbeer, Siegfried. 2008. "The Nordic Region—a Peaceful and Cosy Society?" In *Copyright Norden. The Nordic Model—Fact or Fiction?*, edited by Jesper Schou-Knudsen and the Nordic Council and Nordic Council of Ministers' Communications Department, 59–64. Copenhagen: Nordic Council and Nordic Council of Ministers.

Thorsen, Lotte Rustad. 2011. *Høy deltakelse i Norden*. Oslo: SSB. http://www.ssb.no/ssp/utg/201105/12/. Accessed August 2, 2013.

Thue, Lars. 2006. *Nye forbindelser: 1970–2005*. Norsk telekommunikasjonshistorie, vol. 3. Oslo: Gyldendal Fakta.

Thussu, Daya K. 2006. *International Communication: Continuity and Change*. 2nd ed. London: Hodder Arnold.

TNS Gallup. 2011. "Nøkkeltall mobil og mediebrett." http://www.tns-gallup.no/?did=9099681. Accessed April 9, 2012.

TNS Gallup. 2012. "Internett årsrapport 2012. Offisielle tall fra TNS Gallups internettundersøkelser." www.tns-gallup.no/arch/_img/9105465.pdf. Accessed November 30, 2013.

Tolonen, Kristian. 2011. "22.07.2011 Publikum og Mediebruk." Paper presented at Folks Medievaner 2011, Felix Konferansesenter, Aker Brygge, Oslo, September 14.

Tommila, Päivö, and Raimo Salokangas. 2000. *Tidningar för alla. Den finländska pressens historia*. Göteborg: Nordicom.

Tracey, Michael. 1998. *The Decline and Fall of Public Service Broadcasting*. Oxford: Oxford University Press.

Tryon, Chuck. 2009. *Reinventing Cinema: Movies in the Age of Media Convergence*. New Brunswick, NJ: Rutgers University Press.

Turkle, Sherry. 1995. *Life on the Screen: Identity in the Age of the Internet*. New York: Simon & Schuster.

Turow, Joseph. 2011. *The Daily You: How the New Advertising Industry Is Defining Your Identity and Your Worth*. New Haven, CT, and London: Yale University Press.

Ulset, Svein, and Paul N. Gooderham. 2000. *Internasjonalisering av Telesektoren: Generelle lærdommer og spesielle utfordringer for Telenor*. Bergen: Stiftelsen for samfunns- og næringslivsforskning.

United Nations Development Programme. 2011a. "Human Development Report 2011. Sustainability and Equality: A Better Future for All." New York: UNDP. http://hdr.undp.org/en/reports/global/hdr2011/. Accessed February 15, 2013.

United Nations Development Programme. 2011b. "21 Years of Human Development Reports." New York: UNDP. http://hdr.undp.org/en/reports/. Accessed February 15, 2013.

Vaage, Odd F. 2009. *Kultur- og mediebruk blant personer med innvandrerbakgrunn. Resultater fra Kultur- og mediebruksundersøkelsen 2008 og tilleggsutvalg blant innvandrere og norskfødte med innvandrerforeldre*. Oslo and Kongsvinger: Statistik sentralbyrå.

Vaage, Odd F. 2011. *Norsk mediebarometer 2010*. Oslo and Kongsvinger: Statistisk sentralbyrå.

Vaage, Odd F. 2012. *Norsk mediebarometer 2011*. Oslo and Kongsvinger: Statistisk sentralbyrå.

Van Dijk, Jan. 2006. *The Network Society: Social Aspects of New Media*. 2nd ed. London: Sage.

VGNett. 2009. "VGNett mest lest—noensinne!" http://www.vg.no/nyheter/innenriks/artikkel.php?artid=546528. Accessed January 23, 2012.

VGNett. 2013. "Siv svarte uklart om den norske modellen." http://www.vg.no/nyheter/innenriks/valg-2013/artikkel.php?artid=10116928. Accessed September 24. 2013

Vike, Halvard. 1996. "Norden." In *Fjern og nær: Sosialantropologiske perspektiver på verdens samfunn og kulturer*, edited by Signe Howell and Marit Melhuus, 533–57. Oslo: Ad Notam Gyldendal.

Voltmer, Katrin. 2008. "Comparing Media Systems in New Democracies: East Meets South Meets West." *Central European Journal of Communication* 1 (1): 23–40.

Von Krogh, Torbjörn, and Lars Nord. 2011. "Sweden: A Mixed Media Model under Market Pressures." In *The Media for Democracy Monitor: A Cross National Study of Leading News Media*, edited by Josef Trappel, Hannu Nieminen, and Lars Nord, 265–88. Göteborg: Nordicom.

Vowe, Gerhard. 1999. "Medienpolitik zwischen Freiheit, Gleichheit und Sicherheit." *Publizistik* 44 (4): 395–415.

WAN. 2005. "World Press Trends 2005." *World Association of Newspapers*. Paris: Zenith Optimedia.

Waters, John K. 2010. *The Everything Guide to Social Media*. Avon, MA: Adams Media.

Webster, James G., and Thomas B. Ksiazek. 2012. "The Dynamics of Media Fragmentation: Public Attention in an Age of Digital Media." *Journal of Communication* 62:39–56.

Weibull, Lennart, and Åsa Nilsson. 2010. "Four Decades of European Newspapers:

Structure and Content." In *Media, Markets and Public Spheres. European Media at the Crossroads*, edited by Jostein Gripsrud and Lennart Weibull, 39–70. Bristol: Intellect.

Wikipedia. 2012. "Television Licence." http://en.wikipedia.org/wiki/Television_licence. Accessed March 13, 2013.

Williams, Raymond. 1968. *Culture & Society: 1780–1950*. Harmondsworth: Penguin.

World Economic Forum. 2012. "The Global Information Technology Report 2011–2012." http://www3.weforum.org/docs/Global_IT_Report_2012.pdf. Accessed August 2013.

Ytreberg, Espen. 2001. *Programskjemaarbeid i NRK Fjernsynet: beslutningsprosesser i et maktsentrum*. Rapport nr. 40, Oslo: Institutt for medier og kommunikasjon.

Index